English Constitutional History

Oxford Paperbacks University Series
include many books previously published in
the Home University Library, founded in 1911

OPUS 16 *Oxford Paperbacks University Series*

S. B. CHRIMES

English Constitutional History

Fourth Edition

London
OXFORD UNIVERSITY PRESS
New York Toronto
1967

Oxford University Press, Ely House, London W. 1
GLASGOW NEW YORK TORONTO MELBOURNE WELLINGTON
CAPE TOWN SALISBURY IBADAN NAIROBI LUSAKA ADDIS ABABA
BOMBAY CALCUTTA MADRAS KARACHI LAHORE DACCA
KUALA LUMPUR HONG KONG TOKYO

First edition in the Home University Library 1948
Reprinted 1949
Second edition 1953
Reprinted 1955, 1958, *and* 1960
Third edition 1965
Fourth edition in Oxford Paperbacks University Series 1967

PRINTED IN GREAT BRITAIN AT THE UNIVERSITY PRESS, OXFORD
BY VIVIAN RIDLER, PRINTER TO THE UNIVERSITY

Contents

Prefatory Note to the Fourth Edition

THIS BOOK WAS ORIGINALLY WRITTEN during the reign of King George VI, and Chapter 1 consequently refers to the King, His Majesty's servants, etc. All that is written in this part of the book regarding the King and his place in the Constitution applies equally to a Queen Regnant, and should therefore be so applied during the reign of Her Majesty Queen Elizabeth II.

Opportunities were taken in previous editions to amend and revise the text in various particulars, and to add to the bibliographical notes at the end of the volume. For this edition further correction has been limited mainly to taking into account very recent legislation, such as the several Ministers of the Crown Acts, 1964–5.

S. B. C.

University College, Cardiff
May 1966

Introduction: the Eternal Problem of Government and the English Solution

THE FUNDAMENTAL PROBLEMS OF GOVERNMENT, like most of the really basic problems of human existence, do not change. They remain essentially the same in all ages and in all places. Since the remote, prehistorical times when men first sought to improve their hard lot by establishing civil government of some kind—how, when, or where, no one can say—the fundamental problems involved must have been present, however dimly realized, as they are still present today. These problems, then as now, are essentially how to reconcile apparently opposite aims and ideals. How to reconcile, without constant resort to force, law with liberty, progress with stability, the State with the individual; how to bind the government in power to law of some kind; how to reconcile government, strong enough to be effective, with the consent of at least the majority of the governed: these are the fundamental problems, always existent, always in the nature of things demanding solution.

It is not the problems that change; it is the solutions to them that vary from age to age and from place to place. An infinite variety of solutions has been propounded in the course of human history. Solutions deemed satisfactory, or at any rate tolerated, in one age or in one place, do not satisfy or are not tolerated in another age or in another place. One age or one place will view the problems in different lights from those in which they are viewed in a different age or place. Emphasis on one side of the apparent irreconcilables shifts according to circumstances. Periods of disorder tend to emphasize the importance of law, stability, and the State, as against liberty, progress, and the individual; periods of security and peacefulness tend to weight the balance on the opposite side. In some ages and places, the very notions of liberty and progress barely exist at all, and this circumstance is naturally reflected in the current solutions of the problems. But every age and every place must, consciously or unconsciously, find a solution. The solution which a State does find or possess, so far as the framework of government is concerned, is called its Constitution.

Among the countless Constitutions that have been brought into existence in the world since civil government first began, and of which we have any knowledge, that evolved in England seems to be the most remarkable, and to offer the most successful and most enduring solution to the eternal problems.

The English Constitution is remarkable for many reasons. Alone among existing Constitutions it is the product of a history never entirely broken over a period of some fourteen centuries. Notwithstanding its long history, it is in the highest degree adaptable to the needs of changing circumstances and conditions. The balance between the apparent irreconcilables which is enshrined within it is highly adjustable. The Constitution is resilient to the most extreme pressures put upon it, even the pressure from external enemies. It has survived, without material injury, the dire strain and deadly perils of total war.

It is remarkable also in having been exported wholesale, often more or less *en bloc*, to distant lands, and imitated in greater or less degree by numerous foreign States near and far. The only radically different type of Constitution in the world which can claim anything like comparable success—that of the United States of America—was itself in origin partly an imitation, even if largely based upon misconception, of the English Constitution of the eighteenth century. In the course of the nineteenth and twentieth centuries, it was exported to the Dominions of Canada, Australia, New Zealand, and South Africa. It has been adopted in varying degrees by many of the numerous countries overseas which have under its aegis attained self-government within the Commonwealth, not always very successfully or completely. It was, despite much effort to the contrary, an essential source for the brand-new Constitution of Eire. It has been a model for many States which have in modern times sought to establish a Constitution of a representative and democratic type, but its successful operation depends upon a degree of political maturity not always within the reach of some communities.

It can claim to be not only remarkable for these and other reasons, but also to be markedly successful and enduring, because it succeeds in providing strong and effective government based upon a maximum measure of general consent, whilst at the same time being readily adjustable to changing needs and circumstances.

In short, the English have made permanently important contributions to the solution of the eternal problems of government.

Just as some peoples of the past are renowned still for their contributions to human achievements, such as Greece in the sphere of art, literature, and philosophy; Rome in the sphere of law; Israel in religion; so England, we may surmise, will be identified with the art and practice of government in ages yet to come.

It is the purpose of the following pages to show in broad outline what the English Constitution is now, and how past ages have contributed to it.

1

The Constitution of England

Introductory

THE CONSTITUTIONAL LAW AND PRACTICE of England today is a large theme, and even general accounts of it fill volumes of considerable size. Many able expositions of it have been produced by lawyers and other experts, and some of these are of great weight and authority, but there is no exposition of it which is authoritative and binding in the legal sense. There is no document or statement to which we can point and say, 'This is the English Constitution', as one may in many countries which possess what is called a 'written constitution'. The Constitution of the United States, for example, is the document promulgated in 1787, together with the twenty-two amendments subsequently made to it. Most countries in Europe possess, or until recently have possessed, documents which set out in black and white most, if not all, of their constitutional law. It is true that most countries inevitably develop in the course of the practical working of government certain usages which are not in fact parts of the law in the ordinary sense, but which are found by experience to be indispensable for the smooth working of the Constitution, so that it is doubtful whether any mature Constitution can be said to be wholly written in a legal and authoritative sense.

But in England there is no one document which pretends to set down even the legal, let alone the non-legal or conventional, usages. English constitutional law has to be searched for in a number of different sources. Important parts of it are to be found scattered up and down the statute-book, contained in Acts of Parliament. Thus *Magna Carta*, originally promulgated in 1215, long before anything like a parliament had come into existence, was eventually (1297) enrolled on what came to be known as the statute-book and, except in so far as it has been repealed by later legislation, is still valid law. To take another example, the title to the Crown today is determined by the Act of Settlement of 1701, as modified by the Abdication Act of 1936. The relations between the House of Lords and the House of Commons, at least in certain respects, are laid down in the Parliament Acts of 1911 and 1949. Numerous other examples might be quoted, and obviously our constitutional law is in part written in the statute-book.

But by no means all, or even the greater part, of the law applied in the courts is to be found in Acts of Parliament. A very great deal of it is law not enacted by any legislature at all, but is the common law hammered out through the ages by the King's justices, which provides a source of law in decided cases. This common law consists of judicial decisions on actual cases decided in court, and is to be found written in the reports of proceedings in the courts. Inevitably in the course of litigation many important points of constitutional law have been decided by the justices. Such decisions are binding in the courts as case-law, unless and until they are upset by the decisions of a superior court or by an Act of Parliament. Very many matters of great constitutional importance are common-law matters. The whole of the law of the royal prerogative, except in so far as modified by statute, is common law. The very fact that all courts are bound by Acts of Parliament and must apply them is but a rule of common law; there has never been any legislation ordering the King's justices to enforce statutes or Acts of Parliament. But they do so, and have always done so, or at any rate since a short period of doubt and difficulty in the earliest days of parliamentary enactment. Similarly, innumerable points of great importance to the preservation of the rights and liberties of the individual citizen, and of his remedies if aggrieved, exist only at common law, not by virtue of parliamentary enactments, which, especially in recent times, tend to curtail individual rights rather than to preserve or extend them.

Furthermore, a great many of the rules and usages of the English Constitution are not legal in character, and are not to be found written in the statute-book nor in the reports of judicial decisions, nor written at all, except in the legally unauthoritative, purely academic expositions of scholars, lawyers, publicists, and the like. Many of these rules and usages are of the utmost importance, and if they did not exist or were not commonly observed, the Constitution would be something entirely different from what in fact it is. For example, the whole of what we understand by the Cabinet system rests upon rules and practices that have no legal force. There is no law relating to the Cabinet system as such. The subtle and complex relations between the Cabinet and the Crown, and between the Cabinet and the House of Commons, are quite unknown to the law. The law of the land would be in no way infringed if, for example, a government failed to resign or to procure a dissolution of parliament on being defeated in the Commons—at any rate not by that failure in itself. The law could not be invoked if the King flatly refused to accept the advice of the Cabinet. All these matters, and many others of the very essence of the modern Constitution, are altogether outside the cognizance of the law.

These non-legal rules and usages are usually called the 'conventions' of the Constitution. The name is not perhaps a very satisfactory one, but it serves as well as any that can be proposed. It is not easy to define or to explain these conventions; opinions differ as to their genesis and nature, and as to the sanctions by which they are normally upheld in practice. It has been thought that conventions are respected because, if they were not, breaches of the law itself would inevitably ensue. This is true enough of some conventions. If, for example, a Ministry failed to resign or to dissolve at the behest of a hostile House of Commons, it could not for long carry on government without breaking the law, because it could not lawfully obtain sufficient funds without parliamentary grant.

But it is certainly not true of many other important conventions. No law would be broken, for example, if a Ministry defeated in a general election declined to resign before the new House of Commons had actually assembled and proceeded to pass a vote of no confidence; Ministers could legally continue to draw their not inconsiderable salaries for perhaps an appreciable time. But in fact since 1868 it has been the normal practice for a Ministry to resign forthwith on defeat at a general election, and it is justifiable to regard this practice as an established convention, except in circumstances which suggest that an alternative government cannot immediately be formed. Why should this be so? It is hard to say, except that it is a usage dictated by common sense and the Englishman's normal unwillingness, in matters of moment, to beat about the bush. Conventions are, after all, only rules, usages, or practices commonly recognized by responsible opinion as being the most sensible and reasonable courses to adopt in the circumstances, having regard to the general desire to avoid unnecessary friction and fuss in the working of government. Circumstances frequently recur, and courses found to command general assent on one occasion are usually resorted to again when the same or similar circumstances arise; and so an expedient becomes usage, and usage becomes more or less a rule, the infringement of which would expose a government to the charge of being 'unconstitutional'—a charge which no government will lightly face, for no charge is more likely than this to sap public confidence, and therefore lose the government votes, whether in the House or eventually among the electorate. In a measure, one might almost explain the conventions of the Constitution by saying that they are 'the rules of the game', and leave it at that.

It follows from all this that there is nothing rigid or static about the English Constitution. Not being set out or declared in any sacrosanct document nor hedged in by some special procedure of amendment, it can be changed or modified in any or every particular by the ordinary process of legislation. It can be reformed in any part by an ordinary Act of Parliament assented to in the ordinary way. The judges may add to or perhaps modify the law by their decisions in fresh cases. Conventions may be created by new circumstances and understandings. All these things happen and will doubtless continue to happen. In these ways the English Constitution adapts itself to changing needs and conditions, thus retaining its flexibility and maintaining the principles of organic growth.

It will not surprise most readers to learn that English constitutional law and practice, venerable in many respects, modern in other respects, as it is, incorporating, as it does, the wisdom of centuries of experience and the results of countless experiments in the art and craft of government, is a complex body of many parts and pieces. Some parts—non-essential parts—are a trifle archaic; much of it is not very logical nor very tidy. The strains and stresses of past conflicts and needs have left their mark upon parts of it. A vast mass of intricate relationships between different parts, and a host of matters of subsidiary importance, have to be provided for. But the essence of the matter can, and should be, expressed quite briefly.

The essence of the Constitution today is the temporary entrusting of great powers to a small Cabinet or body of ministers (who are members of one or other of the Houses of Parliament) who are formally appointed to office by and dismissible by the King, but who are politically responsible to the electorate, through the House of Commons, which is periodically elected on a wide, popular franchise, and who are legally responsible under the law, and who are served by a corps of permanent civil servants.

The short preceding paragraph contains the essential formula of the Constitution, and embodies the great secret of responsible government.

The magic formula, which better than any other reconciles the apparently irreconcilable fundamentals, was the fruit not of any theoretical speculation or of any profound foresight, but of long experience of what works and what does not, and of a ceaseless effort to eliminate friction in the actual working of government. Bit by bit, friction in the operations of government was eliminated, and in time—as usual, a long time after the event—the Englishman woke up to the fact that he had achieved—as usual, unconsciously and very slowly—something remarkable and unique. He had achieved a form of government which in the main satisfied him, and which became an object of envy, emulation, and imitation by other people whose experience, for one reason or another, had produced less satisfactory results.

A simple formula, it may seem—to some it will, with justice, seem over-simplified. Yet during the course of fourteen hundred years of English history, some twelve centuries passed before this formula emerged. Conscious possession of the formula is even now less than one hundred years old,[1] and emphasis on parts of it has changed a good deal during the last fifty years; almost certainly it is changing somewhat in front of our eyes at the present time, but we are so near to it that we cannot see it very clearly. Of course, the ingredients in the formula have been a-cooking and a-simmering, some throughout the fourteen hundred years, others for longer or shorter periods, and it is only the mixture of them in certain nice proportions that produces the result as we know it. We must look at the ingredients and the proportions in more detail for further apprehension.

[1] The first intelligible published account of Cabinet government in a modern sense is that by Walter Bagehot in *The English Constitution* (1865). It might, however, be said that the essential principles were clearly understood by Lord Durham in his famous Report on the government of Canada (1839).

His Majesty: The King and the Crown

Government is officially and legally His Majesty's Government, and this expression embodies the whole gist of English Constitutional History as well as forcefully reminding us that the keystone in the structure of the Constitution remains, as always,[1] the Crown.

The King is by law, as by nature, a mere mortal man, but the Crown has become impersonal, immortal, and a symbol of ultimate unity and continuity of purpose in governance, a perpetual reminder that above and beyond all the ephemeral strife and clamour of daily political life there remains the everlasting ideal and purpose of government—the welfare of the State. The extraordinary genius of the English for combining idealistic forms with practical substance is nowhere more apparent than in the modern conception of the monarchy and its place in the constitutional scheme.

From the purely legal standpoint, the King is a natural person who possesses a number of rights and powers (not vested in any other person), some by virtue of royal prerogative (i.e. by common law relating to the King), some by virtue of Act of Parliament, and the sum total of these rights and powers constitutes the Crown. Some of these rights and powers—some of the royal prerogatives—are not very precisely defined, and retain that element of discretion without which government cannot, in the last resort, be carried on.

Nearly all—but hardly quite all—the powers of the Crown today are exercised by or on the advice of the Ministers of the Crown, who in addition exercise more extensive even if not necessarily more vital powers conferred upon them or their Departments direct by Acts of Parliament. The most important powers and functions inherent in the royal prerogative, from the constitutional point of view, concern the relations between the King and Parliament, and between the King and his Ministers.

The royal assent is necessary for Bills passed by the Houses of Parliament before they can become Acts or statutes. The King is the third partner in the legislature. Parliament was itself of royal creation in origin, as will be seen later.[2] In the earlier days of parliamentary history, the King was entirely free to decline to assent to legislative proposals, and refusals were common. In those days, when King and government were indistinguishable,

[1] Except during the Interregnum, 1649–60.

[2] See below, p. 75.

the royal assent or veto was often given by the King in person, but in more recent times it has been usual for the royal assent to be expressed by commissioners appointed specifically for that purpose by the King. In the days when Parliament was in the making, the normal language of the court and of government circles was French, and the royal will was naturally expressed in that language. With that remarkably felicitous habit of the English in preserving ancient memories, especially those which embody a touch of drama and poignancy, the formula of royal pleasure is still to this day expressed in the same foreign words as of old. The assent is given to a public non-financial Bill in the form, *Le Roy le veult* ('the King wishes it'). In the case of a finance bill (granting revenue to the Crown), the time-honoured formula is *Le Roy remercie ses bons sujets, accepte leur benevolence et ainsi le veult* ('the King thanks his good subjects, accepts their benevolence, and so wishes it'). If the Bill is of a private and not a public character, the assent takes the form of *Soit fait comme il est desiré* ('Let it be done as it is desired'). In the days when a Bill was vetoed, the refusal was politely intimated by the words, *Le Roy s'avisera* ('The King will consider it'). This formula has not been used by the Crown since Queen Anne vetoed a Scottish Militia Bill in 1707, but it is rash to say (as some do) that the right of veto is dead. It is not impossible to imagine circumstances in which the King might be justified in refusing to assent to a Bill. A fanatical and impetuous government (if any such can be imagined in England) might conceivably some day force through Parliament measures to which the bulk of the electorate were clearly hostile, and which might imperil the State. If this very improbable contingency arose, there would for the moment be no means of preventing such a measure from becoming the law of the land, except by the exercise of the royal veto. In such hypothetical circumstances, there can hardly be any doubt that the King could and should revive the ancient prerogative of the Crown, and refuse assent. The inevitable consequence of such an event would be an immediate dissolution of Parliament, and a general election. Is it to be doubted that, in circumstances of this kind, the electorate would approve the royal discretion, and return to power a new government less fanatical and impetuous? Clearly only in the most exceptional circumstances could the royal veto be exercised nowadays, but if it ever were exercised, obviously it would be without or contrary to ministerial advice.

The royal prerogatives of summoning, proroguing, and dissolving Parliament are normally exercised on the advice of the Cabinet, or at any rate, of the Prime Minister. It is not, however, clear that the right to dissolve is solely a matter for ministerial advice. It is known that Queen Victoria, Edward VII, and George V held the view that they could refuse to dissolve, but it is not so clear that the King may insist on a dissolution, unless perhaps in the most exceptional conditions, such as those envisaged above. Undoubtedly a veto would be followed by a dissolution. Equally undoubtedly, it is the King's duty to ensure that his government is carried on, and if the state of the House were at any time such that no government could be formed, presumably it would rest with the King to dissolve, with or without advice. It is not easy to imagine other circumstances in which the King could properly insist on a dissolution. Any exercise of the royal prerogative without ministerial advice must necessarily bring the Crown into acute political controversy, and could be justified only (*a*) in a matter of extreme gravity and (*b*) by moral certainty that an alternative government prepared to support the royal action would be formed without delay.

There is one other vital royal prerogative in the exercise of which there may be no ministerial advice available. A new Prime Minister has sometimes to be chosen. The practice today, on a change of Ministry, is for the King to commission a person to form an administration, and the persons selected by this Prime Minister to be Ministers are normally accepted and appointed to office by the King. But whom exactly is the King to commission to form a government? Who is to be Prime Minister? Usually the choice is obvious—it must be the leader of the Party enjoying a majority in the Commons. But there may be no Party with a clear majority in the Commons, or the Party in the majority may for the moment have no obvious leader, or no leader eligible for the office. In these circumstances the King must make the choice himself, with the aid of such advice as he can get. The Cabinet having resigned, there is no government in existence to give him official advice; the retiring Prime Minister may and usually does give advice, which may be good or bad, and in any case is certainly not binding. The King must decide for himself. Thus, when Mr. Neville Chamberlain resigned in May 1940 he himself was still officially leader of the Conservative Party, which still commanded a large majority in the House, but he was obviously not eligible for reappointment.

The process by which the choice of Mr. Winston Churchill was made was far from simple; doubtless it was partly at least due to the final advice of the retiring Prime Minister, partly also to a reasonable estimate of who could best form a government likely to be supported by all parties. Certainly Mr. Churchill could not at that time have been regarded as the leader of the Party, and he was not, it seems, the first preference of either Mr. Chamberlain or George VI.

A different sort of choice had to be made in 1922 on Mr. Bonar Law's resignation. The Conservative Party's majority was not in doubt, but who was going to be the leader of it? More than one person had claims, and in the end a choice had to be made between Lord Curzon and Mr. Baldwin. Advice was taken in various quarters, but the responsibility for the final choice of Mr. Baldwin was necessarily the King's.

Apart from these several possible or actual contingencies, all the official acts of the Crown must by convention be on the advice of the Cabinet, or Ministers. By this means the Crown is kept above politics, and the Ministry made politically responsible, not to the Crown, but to Parliament. That is not to say that the King is necessarily reduced to the position of an automaton. The King is in a position to, and has the right to, discuss matters with his Ministers, and to be informed by them of the facts and state of public business. He regularly and frequently receives the Prime Minister in private audience. He receives copies of Cabinet agenda and conclusions and of diplomatic dispatches, and is made aware of parliamentary proceedings—and all this information is available to him for life, not merely during some comparatively short tenure of office, as in the case of his Ministers. He is thus in a strong and unequalled position to advise, criticize, and warn his transient Ministers, and this is no negligible factor in government. What it all amounts to in practice must obviously vary greatly from time to time, and be dependent upon all the relevant circumstances. No Prime Minister is likely to reveal in detail what he owes to royal advice and guidance, but it is a reasonable assumption that beneficial relations of this kind have existed, especially when the Prime Minister is inexperienced and new in office, and the King is experienced and has been in his office much longer than the Prime Minister has been or is ever likely to be.

Several other powers of vital importance are vested in the Crown by prerogative, and can legally be exercised by the Crown (in practice, by H.M. Government) without reference to Parliament. The declaration of war and peace, the conclusion of treaties with other States, the recognition of other States and governments, the appointment of diplomatic representatives—all these are prerogatives of the Crown, but naturally in modern conditions the most important of them are not exercised without some reference to Parliament.

In addition, the King is the fountain of justice, and in theory is present in every court of the realm; all criminal prosecutions are initiated by the Crown, and can be stopped only by the Crown acting through its law officers. The Crown alone can pardon, acting through the Secretary of State for Home Affairs. The King is Commander-in-Chief of the Armed Forces, titular Governor of the Church as by law established, and is the fountain of honour, the Crown alone being able to create peerages and award honours and decorations, acting in this regard mostly on the advice of Ministers.

Legally, the King can do no wrong, but his Ministers and other servants can and sometimes do. It is common-law doctrine that the King cannot be presumed to have concurred in a wrong, and therefore servants of the Crown who commit a wrong cannot plead the Crown in justification. The King cannot be sued or held legally responsible, but Ministers and civil servants individually can be and are. Government Departments, except in a few minor instances specifically provided for by statute, could not, until recently, be sued. Before 1948, it was only the individual servant or servants of the Crown who actually authorized or did the wrong from whom remedy could be sought for civil wrongs. Usually such a wrong-doer is a subordinate official not in a position to pay substantial damages, and the aggrieved subject might remain aggrieved even after obtaining a favourable judgment in court. Normally, however, the Crown, by good grace, satisfied such judgments out of its own funds.

Nor was there any legal remedy for breach of contract by the Crown, except by grace. It was possible for an aggrieved contractor to supplicate for a Petition of Right, which could not be granted without the Crown's *fiat justitia*, given on the advice of the Home Secretary. There was no appeal against a refusal of the *fiat*, which, however, was normally granted on a prima-facie cause being shown.

The unsatisfactory and indeed anomalous features of this state of affairs received attention from a Select Committee set up in 1921 for the purpose of considering the whole question. Little was done to reform the law until the enactment of the Crown Proceedings Act, 1947, which at long last radically changed the law in these matters, largely in the light of the recommendations of that Committee. Now Government Departments can be sued in tort (civil wrong) and contract, substantially in the same way as private persons can. Government Departments, however, are not in fact private persons and their functions are not private functions; certain exceptions to their liability and certain departures from normal procedures had therefore to be made. But in general the remedies of the aggrieved subject in this sphere were greatly strengthened and facilitated by the Act of 1947.

Thus by virtue of the ancient prerogatives of the Crown, H.M. Government has some vitally important powers at its disposal, which it can, if it thinks fit, exercise without reference to Parliament. But Parliament has the last word, if it wishes. Any Act of Parliament can destroy, modify, or impliedly supersede any part of the royal prerogative, even though the Crown is not bound except by express words in a statute. Not even Parliament, however, can add to royal prerogative. That is one of the very few things Parliament cannot do. If it adds (as it constantly does) to the powers of the Crown, those powers are necessarily statutory, not prerogative.

And so the Crown remains the keystone in the structure of the Constitution, even though the government is carried on in practice by its servants. Furthermore, who can doubt that, in the very last resort and *in extremis*, it is to His Majesty alone that the people can look for the ultimate guardianship of the Constitution?

His Majesty's Servants: The Cabinet and Ministers of the Crown

Legally speaking, there is still no such thing as the Cabinet, even though statute recognizes the existence of Ministers of senior rank, and prescribes a salary for them.[1] Nor, despite what the newspapers say, does a meeting of the Cabinet ever take place. The meetings of Cabinet Ministers that do occur are summoned as meetings of His Majesty's Servants, and that is what in fact they are.

Cabinet Ministers are invariably sworn in as members of the

[1] Ministers of the Crown Act, 1964. See below, p. 16.

Privy Council, membership of which is also granted as an honorary distinction to persons distinguished in public life generally, and which carries with it the courtesy prefix of 'Right Honourable'. In historical origin, the Cabinet may be said to have sprung from the Privy Council.[1] But nowadays the Privy Council as such has only formal duties to perform, such as the promulgation (not the initiation) of Orders-in-Council, which have the force of law, whether by prerogative or under statutory authority, for which Ministers are in fact responsible. Some of the Committees of the Privy Council, such as the Judicial Committee, which is the most important of them and is the final court of appeal from the King's courts overseas and ecclesiastical courts at home, still have major functions of their own to perform.

But, apart from the individual membership of Ministers, there is no connexion today between the Privy Council and the Cabinet. It is the Prime Minister (whose office is also known to the law only in the slightest degree[2]) who determines which of the Ministers of the Crown shall be summoned to meetings of His Majesty's Servants, i.e. be Cabinet Ministers. Practice in this matter of the composition of the Cabinet varies somewhat according to circumstances. During the War of 1939–45 it was found desirable to set up a very small War Cabinet comprising only half a dozen or so of the Ministers responsible for the most fundamental and far-reaching matters, e.g. foreign affairs, finance, and labour, or responsible for no departmental matters at all. Normally, however, the Cabinet has round about twenty members.

In December 1965 twenty-three Ministers were in the Cabinet. In addition to the Prime Minister, nine Secretaries of State (for various Departments) were included, together with the Lord Chancellor, the Lord President of the Council, the Lord Privy Seal, the Chancellor of the Exchequer, the Chancellor of the Duchy of Lancaster, the President of the Board of Trade, and the Ministers of Housing and Local Government; Labour; Technology; Agriculture, Fisheries, and Food; Power; Transport; and Overseas Development. Although the size of the Cabinet has not greatly increased in recent years, the number of other Ministers has increased materially. Salary provision is now made for up to

[1] See below, p. 130.

[2] The Prime Minister's office is mentioned in the Chequers Estate Act, 1917, the Physical Training and Recreation Act, 1937, and the Ministers of the Crown Acts, 1964–5.

nine Secretaries of State, nineteen Ministers of State, and forty-nine lesser or junior Ministers of one category or another, including thirty-six Parliamentary Secretaries.

Recent legislation[1] has not only increased the possible number of Ministers, but has also substantially revised their salaries. The Prime Minister and First Lord of the Treasury now receives £14,000 a year (£4,000 of it tax-free), and is entitled to a pension of £4,000 a year. The Lord Chancellor, who also presides over the House of Lords, has £14,500 a year and a pension of £6,250. Other Ministers for salary purposes fall into three main categories: the holders of the twenty-two senior posts (nearly all of whom are in the Cabinet) receive £8,500 a year; two in a small intermediate category have £5,625 a year, the Parliamentary Secretary (who acts as Chief Government Whip), and the Financial Secretary, to the Treasury; and those in a large category, mostly Parliamentary Under-Secretaries of State or Parliamentary Secretaries, are paid £3,750 a year. The Law Officers of the Crown, who at one time were remunerated partly on a fee basis, have for many years received consolidated salaries, fixed now at £13,000 for the Attorney-General, £9,000 for the Solicitor-General (England and Wales), £8,000 for the Lord Advocate, and £5,625 for the Solicitor-General (Scotland). All Ministers, of whatever grade, are entitled to claim, if they are members of the House of Commons, a taxable allowance of £1,250 a year.

Normally, Ministers must be members of one or other of the Houses of Parliament; this is not legally requisite, but is essential to the Cabinet system. The allocation of Ministers between the two Houses is no longer determined by legislation, except that not more than ninety-one Ministers may sit in the House of Commons. The remaining Ministers at any given time must therefore normally be peers.

However tenuous the legal position of the Cabinet may be, in fact it is today the motive power and source of initiative in government. The ultimate decision on all questions of policy rests with the Cabinet. The Government's general policy, the most important points of Departmental policy upon which individual Ministers are unable or unwilling to decide for themselves, or among themselves, are referred to the Cabinet—or one of its Committees—for discussion and decision. Conclusions therein reached are binding upon all members of the Ministry and of the

[1] Ministerial Salaries Consolidation Act, 1965.

Departments, and the secrecy of its proceedings is maintained by the Privy Councillor's oath and the Official Secrets Acts. It is the duty of Ministers and civil servants to do the best they can to carry such conclusions into effect.

Parliament, and individual members of it, can initiate very little legislation nowadays. In fact, civil servants can and do initiate far more than members of parliament, and often more than Ministers personally do. But of course no civil servant can succeed in initiating policy unless the Minister personally approves of it, and is prepared to face the House of Commons on it. This is not a task to be lightly undertaken, for the House is ever eager to debate and criticize the policies and acts of the Government. The Leader of His Majesty's Opposition (who under the Ministers of the Crown Act 1937 as amended is paid a salary of £4,500 a year by the State[1]) and his supporters will not be slow to criticize in Parliament and outside it every aspect of His Majesty's Government's activity (or lack of activity), nor to put down on the order-paper searching questions to Ministers. Ministers are not bound to answer these questions, but failure to do so, or the giving of unveracious replies, would be attended with such grave loss of prestige, and would inspire such suspicion, that Ministers always answer, except when to do so would be contrary to the national interest; and as the answers are usually drafted by the civil servants who really know the truth of the matter, a high degree of accuracy and relevance is normally attained. The give-and-take of parliamentary question and answer is of great constitutional importance, and is a daily reminder of the responsibility of Ministers to Parliament. It would be of even greater value if the general level of knowledge and intelligence among members of parliament were higher than it is. A good deal of ministerial, departmental, and parliamentary time is wasted by the answering of foolish, pettifogging, and often badly composed questions put down by members anxious to make a show of perspicacity, but who often reveal only elementary ignorance of administration and public policy. Nevertheless, the question-and-answer procedure may and often does serve to elucidate obscure parts of Government policy, and to ventilate and secure redress of mistakes and legitimate grievances of all kinds.

[1] The Ministerial Salaries Consolidation Act, 1965, also provides an annual salary of £3,750 for the Opposition Chief Whip in the Commons, and of £2,000 and £1,500 respectively for the Leader of the Opposition and Chief Opposition Whip in the House of Lords.

Motions on the adjournment, in which almost any topic, other than legislation, can be discussed, are also valuable for similar purposes.

But members of parliament can initiate little nowadays partly because its time is almost wholly taken up with debating the Government's own proposals, and partly because few of them have sufficient knowledge of the practical realities involved to be able to make concrete and detailed legislative proposals. Interested parties outside the House can and do put proposals into their hands, sometimes with success. But, on the whole, Parliament is strong in criticism, weak in initiative.

So it is, for better or for worse, that most of the initiative comes from the Government, which, so long as it enjoys the support of a substantial majority in the Commons, necessarily retains the whip-hand.

The essential principles upon which Cabinet government rests are quite simple. The Crown is bound in matters of policy to follow the advice of the Cabinet, subject always to the royal right of appointing an alternative government capable of carrying on. But no government is capable of carrying on unless it has the support of a majority in the Commons, so that this support is itself a necessary principle of the system. It follows in turn that the Cabinet and Ministers must in practice be members of one or other of the Houses of Parliament, and mostly of the Commons, otherwise they will not in fact enjoy that support. Furthermore, since His Majesty's Government cannot speak with two voices, the responsibility of the Cabinet is collective.

It follows from the latter principle that a Minister who cannot conceal his difference of opinion with his colleagues must either resign or be dismissed on the recommendation of the Prime Minister. Naturally, in fact many differences of opinion may exist in a Ministry, but in their public expressions and acts Ministers must keep in harmony with the agreed policy of the Cabinet, otherwise the machinery of government becomes unworkable, the Government itself becomes publicly open to ridicule, and may lose the votes of some at least of its supporters in parliament. Better that the dissenting member or members of the Cabinet should be dropped than that a defeat and its dire consequences should be risked![1]

[1] The experiment in the National Government in 1931–2 of allowing Liberal ministers to dissent on protection was inevitably a failure, and ended in the resignation of the dissentients.

Just as the Cabinet has in recent times acquired greater power *vis-à-vis* Parliament, so the Prime Minister has gained power and prestige at the expense of his Cabinet colleagues. The older idea that the Prime Minister is merely *primus inter pares* in the Cabinet has long since gone out of fashion. Thus, for example, his salary, until 1937 equal with that of the ordinary Cabinet Minister, has been more than doubled and is now much greater than that of other Ministers, and he alone can claim a pension on retirement.[1] He alone can recommend the appointment and dismissal of Ministers. Many important rights of patronage are his, including appointments to the highest posts in the civil service. He normally presides over full meetings of the Cabinet, and, like other chairmen of other bodies, he can exercise great influence over the course of the discussion and the conclusions reached, according to his personal abilities and powers of persuasion and tact. Moreover, the trump cards are his. His resignation terminates the whole Ministry; he can recommend a dissolution of Parliament. It is sometimes said that the chief reason for the aggrandizement of the Prime Minister's office in the twentieth century is the tendency of the electorate to vote mainly for or against alternative personages to be Prime Minister, rather than for party programmes or individual members. There is undoubtedly some truth in this, but recent experience suggests that this tendency is on the wane. Probably there is more pertinence in the fact that the other Cabinet Ministers are mostly far busier with their own Departments than their predecessors used to be, and are therefore less capable than they were of detachment and the broad co-ordinating view which are still possible for the Prime Minister to attain. The greater the specialized zeal of the individual Ministers, the greater is the need for an Olympian at their head. But the degree of influence which a Prime Minister in fact exercises must necessarily in the last resort depend upon the personal qualities and experience of the holder of the office, and consequently varies from time to time.

The development of the position of the Prime Minister is one of the outstanding features of recent times. Another development of the present century is a great extension in the powers of the executive as a whole. Not only has it acquired great strength *vis-à-vis* Parliament (a theme better considered later),[2] but Parlia-

[1] The Lord Chancellor's pension is for judicial rather than political services.

[2] See below, pp. 21–25 and 38–42.

ment itself has conferred upon it, from time to time, and is likely to continue to do so on an ever-increasing scale, powers that are definitely legislative and even judicial in character.

It is true that a complete separation of executive, legislative, and judicial functions has never been a feature of the English Constitution, even though various French publicists and the makers of the American Constitution thought that it was. Nevertheless, these functions have for the most part been differently distributed, without much overlapping among them, until the last half-century. The cause of this recent conferment of legislative and judicial powers, within limits, upon His Majesty's Government is not far to seek, but opinion upon the phenomenon itself varies. The cause is simply the vast increase in the scope of the State's activity. In the old days, the State concerned itself with little outside the maintenance of order, defence, foreign relations, and occasional reforms of one kind or another; and the machinery of government for these purposes, if not exactly simple, was on a small scale, and its administration not a matter of any great complexity. But for several generations now, the State (whether for better or for worse is not germane to the present discussion) has on an ever-increasing scale undertaken vast schemes of social and economic reform and regulation, schemes requiring complex and detailed administration and constant interference with the daily affairs of the whole people. During wartime, when extreme urgency and adaptability in government and the mobilization of all the nation's resources are the price of survival, the same phenomenon is even more essential and obvious. Such schemes and efforts as these cannot possibly be debated or even considered in detail on the floor of the House of Commons, nor even in its Committees. Inevitably, therefore, Parliament tends to debate only the general principles of much legislation, and to confer power upon the Government, i.e. Ministers or their Departments, to fill in the details and to provide for difficult cases. Parliament often, that is to say, delegates legislative power to, and confers judicial powers upon, the executive—powers formerly considered to be more appropriate to Parliament or Judiciary respectively.

Numerous Acts of Parliament have been passed conferring powers upon Ministers or their Departments to supplement the provisions of Acts by the issue of Statutory Rules and Orders, whether in the form of Orders-in-Council or of Departmental Regulations or Orders. The Minister is necessarily responsible for either variety, since the function of the Privy Council in promulgating Orders-in-Council is purely formal. So far as bulk is concerned, Statutory Rules and Orders (since 1946 all are known as statutory instruments) nowadays loom very much larger than Acts. In 1920, for example, eighty-two Acts were passed, but 2,473 Statutory Rules and Orders were issued; in 1934, the Acts filled a mere 664 pages, whereas 2,104 pages were required to encompass the Statutory Rules and Orders. The relative proportions of statutes and statutory instruments continue to be similar, and at the beginning of 1956 as many as 8,530 of these instruments were in force.

Little objection in principle can be made to the delegation of legislative powers, where the extent of those powers is clearly defined and confined to the amplification in detail of the general principles set out in the Act itself, and where proper safeguards for the scrutiny of the Orders by Parliament and for review by the courts are maintained, and objection in principle is, in any case, in modern conditions, quite academic. But the position is otherwise when, as has sometimes been the case, these limitations and safeguards are, to say the least of it, imperfectly provided. It is in such cases that serious and well-grounded, even if sometimes somewhat exaggerated, criticism has arisen.[1]

Examples of the delegation of legislative powers are very numerous. The powers granted are sometimes most extensive. Sometimes power to modify previous Acts of Parliament has been granted. On occasion, an Act has provided that an Order made thereunder 'shall have effect as if enacted in the Act', thus making it difficult for the courts to consider the validity of such an Order once it has been made.[2] Sometimes the very pretentious formula that an Order 'shall be conclusive evidence that the requirements of the Act have been complied with and that the Order has been duly made and is within the powers of the Act' has been resorted to.

It is not common for powers of judicial decision proper to be conferred upon Ministers, but the conferment of powers of quasi-judicial decision is frequent.[3] The difference between the two

[1] Cf. Lord Hewart, *The New Despotism* (1929); C. K. Allen, *Bureaucracy Triumphant* (1931), *Law and Orders* (1945); Sir Cecil Carr, *Concerning English Administrative Law* (1941). A clear and concise survey of the whole subject is now available in H. W. R. Wade, *Administrative Law* (1961).

[2] See below, p. 24.

[3] The whole subject was investigated by the Franks Committee, whose valuable

classes of decision may be said to be that the former class settles disputes by the application of law to the facts, and the latter by the application of administrative policy. Judicial decision proper is certainly more appropriate to the judiciary, and the less such powers are conferred upon the executive the better.

Numerous examples of the conferment of powers of quasi-judicial decision exist, but it is not always easy to distinguish between this kind of decision and administrative discretion pure and simple. The dividing line is not in the nature of things very clear, and it is easy for lawyers with little knowledge or understanding of administrative requirements to run to excess in criticizing this development, but since the findings of the Franks Committee (1957) a clearer line between legalistic rigidity and administrative necessity has been laid down and followed.

That these phenomena, the legislative and judicial powers of the executive, have come to stay is certain. What is practical politics is to strengthen the safeguards to maintain sound constitutional principles and the rights of the citizen. Some years ago the Government of the day, disturbed by the amount of criticism rife at these tendencies, appointed a Select Committee to review the whole question, and to report what safeguards were desirable or necessary to maintain the principles of the sovereignty of Parliament and the supremacy of the law. The Committee made a number of useful recommendations, proposing better methods of scrutiny by Parliament, the preservation of the principle of the review of Orders by the ordinary courts, and basic principles under which quasi-judicial decisions should be reached and announced.[1]

At long last, in May 1944, the appointment was agreed to of a Select Committee of the House, charged with the task of scrutinizing every Statutory Rule and Order laid before the House, and of calling the attention of the House to any special features that appear to require consideration. This Scrutiny Committee (as it has come to be called) meets every two weeks and has proved to be markedly successful in achieving its main objectives. Only about two per cent of the numerous instruments scrutinized have been the subject of report to the House. Few of the other excellent

Report (Cmd. 218), published in 1957, has been substantially accepted. A permanent Council on Tribunals was established by an Act of 1958 to make rules and to report on the activities of tribunals.

[1] Report of the Committee on Ministers' Powers (1932), Cmd. 4,060.

recommendations of the Select Committee of 1932 were formally adopted,[1] but undoubtedly its Report and the work of the Scrutiny Committee have had a good effect, and the grosser anomalies in the forms of delegated powers have been less apparent in legislation since that date.

As regards delegated legislation, an important subsidiary safeguard now commonly occurring is that provided by the practice of extensive consultation between Departments and interested groups and parties before Orders are made, but this is not in itself any constitutional safeguard. More important, since the decision of the House of Lords in *Minister of Health* v. *the King*,[2] there are fewer instances of delegated legislation that cannot be made subject to the application of the *ultra vires* rule by the courts, and any excess of power or violation of the principles of natural justice in the exercise of ministerial powers can usually, in the last resort, be checked, even if not initially prevented, by the ordinary courts. But naturally these safeguards are somewhat cumbersome and expensive to operate; and in any event they are curative rather than preventive, and no court can question the exercise of discretion by a Minister or a Department if that discretion is itself *intra vires*. For the best preventive safeguard, therefore, we must rely—for what it is worth—upon the good sense of Ministers and especially of the civil servants, whom above all it behoves to temper their Departmental zeal with a keener appreciation of the possible repercussions of their actions upon constitutional principles as a whole, and to remember that the maintenance of those principles may well in the long run be more in the national interest than the short cut in pursuing the policy of their Department. It remains as important as ever for those traditional watchdogs of constitutional liberties, the common lawyers, to scrutinize extensions of executive power, and to make clear to the ultimate sovereign, the public, the true significance of such developments.

In recent years the scope of ministerial power has, at least potentially, been vastly increased by the nationalization of certain industries and public utilities. It is true that the establishment of monopolies for these industries and utilities in favour of public corporations with statutory powers and duties has not in itself

[1] The Statutory Instruments Act of 1946 makes more uniform the rules for laying Orders before the House, and improves the procedure for the publication of Rules and Orders.

[2] See below, p. 44.

created new Ministers and Departments, but inevitably the rise of each new corporation of this kind increases the potential or actual power of one or other of the Ministers of the Crown. The power of patronage in the form of appointments to or dismissals from the boards of these corporations conferred upon Ministers is very considerable; in most instances a Minister is authorized to give general directions to such corporations, when, in his opinion, the national interest so requires; his consent is required for certain financial and organizational schemes involved. On the other hand, ministerial responsibility is not accepted for the ordinary administration of these undertakings, with the result that, among other things, machinery for ensuring their efficient and economic operation in the public service is either very weak or non-existent. Moreover, the legal duties committed to these corporations are framed in such general terms as to raise doubts whether they could be legally enforced. The public is thus left very much at the mercy of its own corporations, and the constitutional problems arising from the nationalization of industries remain largely unsolved, and are likely to remain so until some issue emerges grave enough to compel a solution.

His Majesty's Civil Servants: Departments of State

Both Ministers and civil servants are equally servants of the Crown, and civil servants are not servants of one another, nor of Ministers. No matter to what lengths hierarchical principles within a Department may be carried—and they are necessarily carried very far—the legal principle of individual service of the Crown remains unaffected. Civil servants[1] are instantly dismissible by the Crown. In practice, however, few things are so permanent as tenure of established posts in the Civil Service. England has happily avoided the 'spoils system', and the personnel of the Civil Service does not change with every change of government. For all practical purposes, therefore, the establishment is permanent, and instances of dismissal for misconduct or conduct considered to be inappropriate are extremely rare. Normally, the civil servant will enjoy, or at any rate retain, his office and emoluments up to the time of his retirement, and thereafter subsist undisturbed on his pension. From the national and constitutional point of view, this permanence of the established

[1] Except for one or two statutory exceptions.

Civil Service, although it may in some degree give cover for inefficiency, is of inestimable advantage. Without it, we might have to endure a Civil Service as amateurish and as transient as many Ministers are, not to mention the evils and corruption inseparable from a political Civil Service. But, like most advantages, it has to be purchased at a cost. The principal cost in this case is the sacrifice of personal political opinions by the civil servants, or at any rate the outward expression of them, and this in its turn means that some of the more robust minds in each generation will not, on any account, enter or remain in the Service. A civil servant who is a die-hard Tory by personal conviction cannot refuse to do his best to carry out the socialist programme of a Labour Minister, nor can the socialistically-inclined civil servant sabotage what he may regard as the reactionary schemes of a Tory Minister. Nor would it be feasible for a government to tolerate public expressions of political opinions and criticisms by civil servants. So that in political questions the Civil Service is a silent service, and its members are, or should be, doomed to anonymity.

Being thus permanent and politically silent, the Civil Service has evolved for itself[1] a quite remarkable code of professional conduct. The civil servant owes undivided allegiance to the State, and he must so conduct himself in both official and private life as to avoid any possible conflict, or appearance of conflict, between the interests of the State and his private interests.[2] The ethical code of the Civil Service has consequently become extraordinarily high, and it is questionable whether any other civilian profession can match the civil servants in their standards of personal integrity, honesty of purpose, and devotion to duty. There can be no doubt that the English Civil Service has a place in the national life transcending its obvious administrative sphere. Its moral example is an abiding factor in the influences that help to shape the national character.

In the constitutional sphere, the civil servants in reality occupy a far more important place than is commonly recognized. Apart from the discharge of often difficult but comparatively routine

[1] The code is, however, partly laid down in statutes, Orders-in-Council, and Treasury rules.

[2] It is to be hoped that the recent repeal of the Trades Disputes Act of 1927, which among other matters removes the ban on the affiliation of civil servants' unions with trade unions having political objects, will not result in any modification of this vital principle.

tasks—the bulk of which is huge under modern conditions—the major functions of the Civil Service, in its higher grades, are two-fold: (*a*) to advise the Minister on all aspects of his tasks as Minister and (*b*) to carry into effect whatever the Minister may decide shall be done.

As regards (*a*), the civil servants help to make, and very often to initiate, policy. Ministers, especially those new to office, very soon find the airy generalities and platitudes of the hustings require very careful thought and perhaps recasting in the form of practicality and actuality before anything 'can be done about it'. Any political project must be converted into terms of administrative feasibility before anything can come of it. It is in this conversion from theory to practice that the civil servant has a powerful, often decisive, influence. He is usually of long experience in the arts of administration; he knows the existing machinery, and is probably expert in some part of it; he can advise to what extent modification or extension of it will be necessary or possible in order to carry out some new policy proposed by the Minister. He may, and frequently does, put forward proposals for the improvement of existing arrangements, proposals which may be sufficiently far-reaching to affect policy, and may require legislation to give them effect. A Minister cannot afford to ignore proposals of this kind, nor any suggestions that may result in enhanced reputation for himself or increased efficiency in the work of his Department. Many such proposals, initiated by civil servants, sometimes by officers in comparatively junior grades, via the Minister's approval and perhaps that of the Cabinet, find their way on to the statute-book or into statutory instruments. By whomsoever initiated, all legislation sponsored by the Government is drafted by expert draftsmen who are civil servants.

Of course, the responsibility for policy rests wholly upon the Minister, who will have to answer for it in Parliament. At debates on important matters, the civil servants will be in 'the box' behind the Speaker's chair, ready to counsel the Minister if need be, through his parliamentary private secretary who acts as a liaison between the floor of the House and the officials' 'box', which is technically outside the House. Few Ministers would care to come to a decision on policy without prior consultation with some at least of the more senior members of their Departments, who in turn will usually find it desirable to consult less senior members who may be more expert in a particular field of administration. Advice given in this way will usually be broadly impartial, and will cover possible objections to, as well as the advantages of, the course proposed. The good civil servant is expert in forecasting the probable repercussions of new measures, and it is part of his duty to protect his Minister from snares and pitfalls; he may on occasion have a hard task in persuading his Minister that a pet scheme is unworkable this side of Utopia. Usually the Minister will be left in no doubt as to the probable difficulties and the possible consequences of his proposal. Thus he is in a position to make a decision (if he can) for himself, in the light of well-informed and honest, unbiased opinion.

Once the Minister has decided on his policy with regard to any matter, the civil servant must loyally carry out that policy, no matter how vigorously he may have opposed it at the discussion stage. He can help to shape the policy, but once the policy is decided, all must do their best to carry it out with complete loyalty and all due energy.

The bulk of the civil servants are occupied, under the supervision of the administrative grade, with the second main function, that of carrying out the Minister's policy. A policy or a general decision may perhaps be set out in a few lines of writing, but to carry it out into effect may require vast masses of detailed planning and hosts of subsidiary decisions, occupying the whole-time labours of numerous civil servants of all grades, perhaps the setting up of new departments, and even the opening up of new offices all over the country, perhaps overseas. All the countless questions involved have to be decided by some officer, and all the correspondence arising has to be dealt with by someone.

The work of modern administration is very exacting, and calls for high qualities of judgement, discretion, and patience, and for not a little ingenuity. Innumerable questions arise in day-to-day business which can and must be settled without delay, and are decided at different levels within the Service. Obviously only the largest and most important matters involving policy are dealt with at the political level, i.e. by the Parliamentary Secretaries or Ministers, or matters likely to lead to immediate repercussions in the House. Most other questions, the interpretation of existing policy, its application to particular cases, the creation and adaptation of administrative machinery and practice to implement agreed policy, will normally be dealt with and decided by the administrative or executive grades, at one level or another according to the importance and nature of the question, and according to the initiative, knowledge, and temerity of the individual civil servant. Practice in this connexion varies widely, and the degree of devolution attained depends mainly upon the personal qualities of the actual persons concerned. These grades have the co-operation, where necessary, of the professional, legal, and scientific grades, and are assisted by the clerical and sub-clerical grades, the telephonists, and others without whom the wheels of the great machine would very soon slow down and come to a stop.

The Minister must accept responsibility for whatever is done by members of his Department, and must answer for it in Parliament if need be. Hence the necessity for caution by civil servants in their daily tasks, and the practice of referring matters to 'higher authority' before committing the Minister to a decision in any matter of special difficulty or doubt. The spectre of the Parliamentary Question haunts the civil servant all his days; he, of all people, is in no danger of forgetting the maternal solicitude of the Mother of Parliaments. Hence the tendency to love and cherish safe precedents, and the committal of nearly everything to writing against the day when someone not-to-be-fobbed-off wants to know why so-and-so was done. Neither the Service nor anyone else is to be blamed for these precautions; they are the inevitable and proper consequence of the principles of ministerial responsibility and the sovereignty of Parliament.

The most obvious defects in the Civil Service today do not arise so much from the individual civil servant as from the organization or lack of organization of the Service itself. On the one hand, the principles of hierarchy are apt to be carried too far; and, on the other hand, there are grounds for believing that the Service is insufficiently unified.

Within each Department there tend to be too many grades in the hierarchy. In a large Department, the administrative grade alone may be represented by as many as six grades, each reporting when appropriate to the rank above. The Assistant Principal reports to the Principal, the Principal to the Assistant Secretary, the Assistant Secretary to the Under-Secretary, he to the Deputy Secretary, who reports to the Permanent Secretary, who is responsible to the Minister. There can be no doubt that a hierarchy of these dimensions results in waste of time and energy and repetition, and discourages the acceptance of maximum responsibility by the less senior grades. Greater economy of effort and public money could be secured, with generally quite as good if not more efficient results, by reduction of this top-heavy hierarchy, and by measures to encourage greater responsibility at lower levels.[1]

The Service as a whole appears to be insufficiently unified. Only in certain respects can there be said to be one Civil Service at all. It is true that H.M. Treasury has a general responsibility and exercises supervision and makes rules regarding such matters as salary scales, conditions of service and retirement, and the like, but in fact most civil servants regard themselves too much as members of a particular Department, and many if not most of them spend the whole of their careers within one Department. Interchange of staff between Departments, although far less rare than it used to be, is still the exception rather than the rule. Consequently, the Service is still essentially a congeries of Departmental staffs, each with its own outlook and foibles, with Departmentalism in all its manifestations as its abiding temptation.

It cannot be pretended that the problems involved in these matters are susceptible of easy solution. It may be doubted, and often is doubted (for reasons of differing merits), whether H.M. Treasury, primarily concerned as it is, or should be, with questions of finance and economy, is really the best instrument for exercising primacy over the Service, which means over the staff of other Departments. It is not easy to see valid arguments in favour of the custom of according the style of Head of the Civil Service (with a slightly higher salary) to the Permanent Secretary of the Treasury. There may even be serious objections to a permanent subordination of the Service as a whole to the financial Department. A more logical and possibly less objectionable arrangement might be for the Headship of the Civil Service to be centred on the Secretary to the Cabinet, and primacy to be focused upon the Cabinet Office, which has already become in effect the Prime Minister's Department, and as such is very probably destined to effective pride of place among Departments. The Cabinet Office alone is, in an administrative as distinct from a financial sense, above all other Departments, and it is perhaps more appropriate that the Civil Service should be centred on the office closest to the Prime Minister rather than on that of the Chancellor of the Exchequer, even though the Prime Minister is the titular First Lord of the Treasury.

[1] A step in the right direction was taken by the decision to abolish the grade of Principal Assistant Secretary (September 1945, Cmd. 6,680).

But the Treasury is the oldest Department of State, whereas the Cabinet Office dates only from 1916, and any re-allocation of precedence, if it ever comes at all, is likely to be remote.[1]

The Departments of State are today very numerous, and are on the increase. No particular purpose would be served by listing all of them here, nor by considering them separately.[2] For each of them one or another Minister of the Crown is responsible, whether he be designated (for historical reasons) Secretary of State, or Minister, or by one of the more individual titles, such as the First Lord, President, Lord Privy Seal, and so on. In most Departments, there are also one or sometimes two junior Ministers, known usually as Parliamentary Under-Secretaries of State or Parliamentary Secretaries, whose main functions are so far as practicable to relieve the Minister of some of his burdens at the political level.

The efficiency of Departments and working conditions and amenities naturally vary a good deal, more than they should, or would, if the unification of the Service were carried further than it is. It does not always occur that the Permanent Secretary is the ablest senior man in the Department, and not all Permanent Secretaries are capable of infusing a spirit of energy and enthusiasm throughout their Departments, nor even of maintaining a good *esprit de corps* and general level of contentment in the ranks. Seniority, as distinct from ability, is still often the only obvious explanation of promotions that are made, especially in the higher ranks, although this state of affairs is less common now than formerly.

But looking at the matter as a whole,[3] and balancing the efficiency attained against the enormity and complexity of the tasks imposed on the Service, and notwithstanding occasional lapses and absurdities, there can be no question but that the State is faithfully served by its civil servants, without whose sustained efforts, skilled intelligence, and often selfless devotion, His Majesty's Government could not be carried on for a single instant.

[1] It should however be noted that recently the offices of Secretary to the Cabinet, Secretary to the Treasury, and Head of the Civil Service have been held for an appreciable time by the same individual.

[2] A very useful list, with explanatory notes on each as then extant, is to be found in W. I. Jennings, *Cabinet Government* (2nd ed. 1951), Appendix III. For the current list, see recent issues of Parliamentary Debates (Hansard).

[3] Without prejudice to the national sport of bureaucracy-baiting.

The King in Parliament: 'My lords and Members of the House of Commons'

On the opening of any session of Parliament, the *Official Report* of the House of Lords begins as follows:

> The King being seated on the Throne, and the Commons being at the Bar with their Speaker, His Majesty was pleased to make a Most Gracious Speech to both Houses of Parliament, and then retired.

On the same occasions, the House of Commons' *Report* reads:

> Mr. Speaker: I have to acquaint the House that this House has this day attended His Majesty in the House of Peers, and His Majesty was pleased to make a Most Gracious Speech from the Throne to both Houses of Parliament, of which, for greater accuracy, I have obtained a copy, which is as followeth: 'My lords and Members of the House of Commons,' etc., etc.

These extracts serve to illustrate the formal relations of the King and Parliament. At the opening of a session, whether of a new or of an old parliament, the King (usually in person) makes from the Throne in the House of Lords a speech which in fact is composed by his Ministers and which sets out their programme of major proposals for the session. Headed by their Speaker, the Commons, who in earlier days were not necessarily part of Parliament at all, merely attend at the Bar of the House of Lords and listen. The King, when during the course of his reading of the speech allusion is made to finance, changes the form of address, drops 'my lords', and addresses only the 'Members of the House of Commons', thus recognizing the supremacy of the Commons in financial matters. After the address the Commons return to their own House, and both Lords and Commons proceed to debate the programme separately.

'The King then retired.' His Majesty never now attends Parliament in person except for this formal opening of the session, unless it be for the giving of the royal assent to bills, which is normally done nowadays by commissioners, or for some very special State occasion. The Throne, however, remains in the House of Lords always, and is symbolic, not only of the past, but also of the present fact that the Crown is the third partner in Parliament.

Of the other two partners, the House of Lords, though for long overshadowed in power by the Lower House, is much the senior, and even now is not by any means a sleeping partner.

The House of Lords is composed today of four different elements, mainly but not wholly hereditary in character. It comprises (1) the hereditary peers and peeresses in their own right, of England, of Scotland, of Great Britain, and of the United Kingdom, who have not disclaimed their peerage,[1] (2) men or women created peers or peeresses for life under the Life Peerages Act, 1958, with rank as barons or baronesses, (3) twenty-six spiritual peers, including the archbishops of Canterbury and of York, the bishops of London, Winchester, and Durham, and twenty-one other bishops of the Church of England in order of seniority and whilst remaining in charge of dioceses, (4) nine Lords of Appeal-in-Ordinary, who hold life peerages only, and who are concerned mainly with the judicial work of the House, the House of Lords being the final court of appeal from courts of justice within the country.

The total number of members of the House of Lords is about 900, but so far as the normal legislative functions of the House are concerned the effective number is much smaller, only about 100 or even fewer of the peers regularly applying themselves to attendance.[2] This effective core consists usually of such hereditary peers as have taste and capacity for the work, together with a number of men distinguished by their own abilities and experience in various walks of life who have been granted peerages. This effective core, therefore, consists mainly of men of high attainments and notable achievements, not necessarily in party politics, whose knowledge of public affairs is extensive, whose public services are distinguished, and whose intellectual attainments are often outstanding. It is not surprising, therefore, that the debates of this effective core are often on a high level, and, not being carried on with a view to future votes and present constituents, frequently surpass in wisdom and disinterestedness the performances in the Commons.

Peerages can be created only by the Crown, normally with the advice of the Prime Minister. There is no limit to the number of possible creations. No new creations in the ancient peerages of England, Scotland, or Ireland are now made; all creations are in the peerage of the United Kingdom. All duly qualified peers who have attained twenty-one years of age, not being aliens, bankrupts, or lunatics, nor serving sentence after conviction, are entitled to a summons to attend Parliament.

[1] See below, p. 35.

[2] Since 1957 peers have been able to claim up to three guineas a day (raised in 1964 to four and a half guineas) as expenses for actual attendance.

The privileges of the House of Lords are very similar to those of the House of Commons, and of these mention will be made later.[1] The ancient individual privilege of trial by fellow peers on charges of treason or felony was abolished in 1948.

For a long time before 1911 the legal powers (apart from the appellate jurisdiction) of the House of Lords were similar to those of the Commons, although in practice for several centuries financial Bills had come to be regarded as the preserve of the Commons. It was departure from this tradition that led to the enactment of the Parliament Act of 1911, which in part fixed the relations between the two Houses and certain other matters. Under its terms, the assent of the Lords remained necessary before Bills could be sent up for the royal assent, except (1) in the case of money Bills certified by the Speaker to be such, provided that such a bill had been sent up to the Lords at least one month before the end of the session, and (2) in the case of any public Bill (other than a Bill to extend the legal duration of a parliament beyond five years) which had passed the Commons in three successive sessions, provided that two years elapsed between the second reading of the Bill in the first of those sessions and the third reading in the third of those sessions. Thus the legislative power of the Lords, in the last resort, did not exceed the ability to delay a money Bill by about a month, and any public Bill (not proposing to extend the duration of parliament) for two years, and to reject altogether a Bill to extend the life of a parliament or any private Bill. But without any except theoretical provocation, the Government of the day took steps, in the Parliament Act, 1949, to reduce from two years to one year the maximum period during which the Lords might delay the enactment of a public non-financial bill. How far even this power will be used in future is open to question.[2] The major source of the weakness of the Lords is not to be found in the Parliament Acts, but in the fact that no government would think it necessary to resign, or to dissolve parliament, no matter how often they might be defeated in the Lords. The speedy result of any such occurrences of that kind, if persisted in to the last ditch, would probably be, not the resignation of the

[1] See below, p. 38.

[2] Only three Bills have so far been enacted without the assent of the Lords: the Welsh Church Disestablishment Act, 1914, which was later amended before becoming operative, the Government of Ireland Act, 1914, which was subsequently repealed before coming into force, and the Parliament Act, 1949.

government, or a dissolution, but the drastic reform of the House of Lords itself.

Most critics in this country agree that a Second Chamber to the legislature is desirable. A Second Chamber provides a forum for weighty opinion that may not find adequate expression in the Lower House, and some brake on the rather impetuous efforts of a popularly elected House is a reasonable precaution in the national interest, which is by no means always identical with Party interest. It is highly desirable that a place should be found in the legislature for men who are not necessarily endowed with those qualities which appeal most to popular electorates. Political wisdom is not exclusively confined to successful performers on Party platforms, and the balance of argument is undoubtedly in favour of preserving a Second Chamber composed on principles different from those upon which a purely elective House rests. Few unbiased critics, however, can pretend that the present composition of the House of Lords, or the position of the House in the scheme of things, is satisfactory. Of all the institutions of government, the House of Lords stands most in need of reform. The difficulty is to get agreement on a sufficiently wide basis as to what reform is appropriate, not to mention the difficulty of any government in being able to find enough time, amid the great pressure of more urgent business, to deal with the problem. A Commission under Lord Bryce was set up in 1917–18 to consider the whole question, but made no official report, and nothing but sporadic and ineffective suggestions have been made since. It is perhaps not difficult to suppose that any reform must be aimed primarily at removing or drastically modifying the hereditary character attaching to present membership of the House, and therefore at legalizing the creation of life peerages or peerages for a term of years for other than judicial purposes. Life peerages for men and women can be created under the Life Peerages Act, 1958, and since the Peerages Act, 1963, an hereditary peerage can be disclaimed irrevocably for life without affecting the succession to it thereafter. Nor is it easy to agree as to the extent of legal power that should be accorded to a reformed House of Lords. But the English genius for compromise and improvisation is far from exhausted, and it is but a question of time for reform to be undertaken.

The House of Commons consists at present of 630 members, elected under universal adult franchise. There is roughly one member for each 60,000 electors, but constituencies are not divided on a purely mathematical basis. Some attempt is made to preserve a certain natural unity in creating constituencies, which in all cases return one member, and are all on a territorial basis.

By the terms of the Representation of the People Act, 1949, any British subject, male or female, of twenty-one years of age, not being subject to one of the legal disqualifications, e.g. not being certifiably lunatic, a convicted person undergoing sentence, a person found guilty of corrupt practices at a previous election, and not being a Returning Officer at the election nor a peer or peeress in her own right other than in the peerage of Ireland, is entitled to be registered as a voter in a constituency, if qualified by residence in the constituency. Provisions are in force for the registration of men and women absent from their constituencies on military service, and, in certain circumstances, for voting by proxy or by post.

In order to vote at all, a person must in fact be registered on the electoral register in the constituency by the due date; otherwise a ballot paper cannot be issued on polling day. The register is prepared by a registration officer, who is normally either the clerk of a county council or the town clerk of a borough. An appeal lies from the decision of a registration officer to the County Court, and on a point of law from the County Court to the Court of Appeal. The local organization of the ballot is the responsibility of a Returning Officer, who is the sheriff, mayor, or chairman of an urban district council, the actual duties being performed normally by the registration officer as acting Returning Officer. Heavy penalties for corrupt practices on the part of anyone in an election, whether candidate, official, or elector, are provided by statute. The ballot is secret,[1] although in fact the preservation of a counterfoil to the ballot paper on which the voter's number on the register is marked makes it possible for a vote and the identity of the voter to be traced. In practice, however, the counterfoils and the ballot papers are never re-assembled, except in the rare cases where the documents are required as evidence of illegal practices.

As all constituencies return one member only, each elector can obviously vote for only one candidate, and election is by simple majority vote. Thus it is theoretically possible for 51 per cent of the whole electorate to secure 100 per cent representation. In practice, so extreme a case can of course rarely occur, but the number of seats obtained by a Party frequently bears very little

[1] Except in the case of votes by proxy or by post.

mathematical proportion to the total number of votes cast for it, and minority Parties may obtain representation far below what would be proportionate to the total number of votes cast in their favour. A good deal of criticism has been levelled at this state of affairs, especially by members of Parties who see very slight prospect of ever securing under it more than insignificant representation. Various schemes for alternative votings and proportional representation, of varying degrees of elaboration, have accordingly been proposed, but fortunately none of these gain any wide support. The English voter so far has shown no enthusiasm for voting mathematically, and is generally wisely content to vote for or against something or somebody, and to leave it at that. As a result, we have been spared the disastrous consequences of a House split up into numerous small Parties and factions, in which no government can hold office without interminable intrigues and unreal coalitions. The English system works best when it throws up a strong Government and a strong Opposition. If the electorate can achieve that result, it can be well content to leave mathematically proportioned voting to more subtly-minded peoples. In England, any minority is free to become a majority—if it can; it takes a long time for this to happen, but it does happen.

Membership of the House of Commons is open to any British subject, male or female, of twenty-one years of age, if not subject to one of the legal disqualifications, such as lunacy (certifiable), bankruptcy, peerage (other than peers of Ireland), or undergoing sentence after conviction. Certain persons are ineligible, e.g. clergy of the Churches of England, Scotland, or of Rome, judges of the Supreme Court, the sheriffs, government contractors, and holders of most paid offices under the Crown, other than ministerial office.[1] Members cannot resign, and can retire only by becoming disqualified, i.e. in practice by being granted on request the sinecure office under the Crown of the stewardship of the Chiltern Hundreds or of the manor of Northstead. Members are entitled to a salary (of £2,000 a year), and may claim a taxable expenses allowance up to £1,250 a year.[2]

The famous privileges of the House are perhaps more important historically than at the present day, except for freedom of speech

[1] The number of Ministers who may sit in the Commons is limited to ninety-one by statute.

[2] A compulsory contributory pension scheme for all Members of Parliament is now in operation.

in the House. Historically, the privileges were the means whereby the House climbed to political power *versus* the Crown, and perhaps may some day be useful again *versus* an overmighty government.

The member of parliament has the privilege of freedom of arrest during the session, except on charges of treason, felony, breach of the peace, and indictable offences generally. He has freedom of speech in the House, and can say what he likes about anything or anybody without legal risks, and the privilege extends to bona-fide reports of speeches in the House. The Commons have the collective right of access through their Speaker to His Majesty, whilst the Lords have the somewhat archaic right of individual access. The House has the right to exclude strangers, i.e. persons who are neither members nor officials of the House, and so can enter into secret session. It can determine the qualifications of its members, but refers disputed elections to the decision of two judges of the High Court. It regulates its own procedure by Standing Orders. It can punish anyone for infringement of its privileges and rules or for contempt, and can commit to prison for the duration of the session (the Lords can commit indefinitely). The courts will not interfere if satisfied that the matter is within the privileges of the House. It may through its Speaker admonish, suspend, or expel any member. But it cannot (without an Act of Parliament) prevent an expelled member from being re-elected.

The House can adjourn itself, but can be prorogued or dissolved only by the Crown. Adjournment and prorogation can only be to a definite date; prorogation stops all current business; dissolution terminates the life of the parliament altogether, and is irrevocable and final.[1] Under the Parliament Acts of 1911 and 1949 the life of a parliament cannot in any event last more than five years.[2]

The functions of the House fall into four main categories, although there are, of course, various other functions which cannot be considered in brief. The first of these main functions is the legislative function. Bills may be introduced by any member (of either House, except that money Bills must originate in the Commons, and there, in practice, only on the recommendation of a Minister), but nowadays few Bills of any importance get very far

[1] Except if a demise of the Crown occurs before a new parliament is elected; in which case the old parliament is revived for six months unless sooner dissolved.

[2] Unless extension is authorized by Act of Parliament, to which the assent of both Houses is necessary.

unless sponsored or initiated by the Government, owing to lack of parliamentary time and to what is regarded as the urgency of the Government programme. It is to be hoped that some day conditions will allow private members to have better opportunities for initiating legislation. Bills may be public or private (not to be confused with Private Members' Bills, which may be either public or private). A Public Bill is one affecting the community generally, whilst a Private Bill is one concerned only with some corporate, local, or individual matter.

The procedure of the House is a large and complicated theme and cannot be discussed here at all, except for a brief indication of the broad outline of procedure on Public Bills, other than money Bills. Before a Bill passes the House, it must pass though three stages or readings. The first reading is purely formal, and amounts to no more than an introduction of the Bill, and its automatic passage through this stage gives authority to print. At the second reading, the general principles of the Bill are debated, and if the motion that 'the Bill be now read a second time' is carried, the Bill is remitted to Committee; but if the motion is amended in any way, the Bill is rejected. After the second reading the Bill is considered in Committee, either by one of the Standing Committees or, in more exceptional cases, by a Committee of the whole House, or by a Select Committee. The proceedings in Committee are less formal than on the floor of the House; members may speak to amendments more than once, and the clauses of the Bill are gone through in considerable detail. The Standing Committees are composed of representatives of most shades of opinion in the House; the Government will have a majority on each Committee, but often finds it expedient to adopt amendments proposed by its own supporters or by its opponents, and Bills often emerge from Committee considerably modified.

The next stage is debate by the House on Report, i.e. on the Bill as amended in Committee, during which further amendments may be made. Thereafter, at the third reading, verbal amendments only may be made, although rejection is still possible. The carrying of the motion that the Bill 'be now read a third time' passes the Bill, and it is then ready for remission to the House of Lords; but if the motion is amended, the Bill is rejected.[1]

[1] Procedure on a Private Bill is different in character, and resembles a semi-judicial proceeding. Thus, at Committee stage, interested parties may be and frequently are represented by counsel, who may call evidence. This procedure is necessarily slow

Obviously, an Act of Parliament ought not to be made lightly or without thorough consideration, and the procedure of the House is well designed, at least in theory, to ensure that Bills are adequately discussed. In practice, however, the position is somewhat less satisfactory, parliamentary time being limited, and congestion of business being a very serious and ever-growing evil. Inevitably, therefore, various expedients have been adopted with a view to curtailing debate and expediting business. Under the 'closure' procedure, any member of the House or of a Committee may move that 'the question be now put', and if carried, this terminates debate. The Speaker or Chairman may refuse to put this motion, if he is of the opinion that the rights of minorities would thereby be infringed. Under 'kangaroo' closures, selected amendments only may be discussed, and there are various 'guillotine' devices, whereby fixed periods of time are allotted for the discussion of the different parts of the Bill or for the various stages, at the end of which the question is put without further debate. The Government, by virtue of its majority, can always, in the last resort, impose these expedients upon the House if it wishes, but normally the arrangements are made by amicable agreement between the Whips on both sides of the House. If agreement on these matters is not reached, the Opposition has the weapon of obstruction, which can be very embarrassing to the Government, notwithstanding the latter's trump-card of the larger battalions in the division lobbies.

After finally passing both Houses, a Bill is ready for submission for the royal assent, and the formula of enactment sets out the legal sanction of an Act of Parliament: 'Be it enacted by the King's most Excellent Majesty, by and with the advice and consent of the Lords Spiritual and Temporal, and Commons, in this present Parliament assembled, and by the authority of the same . . .'

The House normally disposes somewhat summarily of its functions in regard to revenue and expenditure, for which legislation is always requisite. Parliament (in practice, the Commons) alone can authorize the raising of revenue and its expenditure. No money can be raised or expended by His Majesty's Government without the sanction of Parliament, and revenue when raised can

and expensive, and the extensive needs of Local Authorities are met under the Provisional Order procedure, whereby a government department may make an Order on application by a Local Authority, which becomes statutory by inclusion in a Provisional Order Confirmation Act.

be expended only for the purposes so authorized. But in practice nowadays the Commons almost automatically accept the financial proposals of the Government (private members, as distinct from Ministers, are, by the salutary practice of the Houses, prevented from proposing the raising or expenditure of money). The House can and does criticize, sometimes with considerable effect, the Chancellor of the Exchequer's financial proposals (considered in the Committee of Ways and Means, a Committee of the whole House), and also debate items of proposed expenditure (in the Committee of Supply, also of the whole House), but the time available for these debates is almost wholly taken up with general questions of policy, and in almost no degree devoted to detailed matters of finance, economy, and the like. One of the most remarkable and perhaps disquieting features of the present century, as compared with preceding periods, is the reduction of effective parliamentary control (and concern) over finance to a mere formality, whether it be because of lack of time, knowledge, or interest, or of an excessive faith in the wisdom of H.M. Government in disposing of the national income, or merely because proposals for economy nowadays lose rather than win votes. Consequently, parliamentary control over finance has become mainly latent, but it remains, of course, supreme in the last resort. Failure on the part of the Commons to pass the annual Finance Act or Appropriation Act would speedily put any government out of office, for lack of funds. Restriction of expenditure to authorized purposes is ensured by the careful labours of H.M. Treasury and the Comptroller and Auditor-General, on whom, backed by the Public Accounts Committee of the House of Commons, the public has to rely for such efforts at economy as are made.

Apart from these legislative functions, the task of Parliament is to reject, support, criticize, or applaud H.M. Government for the time being. An adverse vote in the Commons on any important matter is bound to bring about the speedy resignation of the Government or a dissolution of Parliament, and even a substantial fall in its majority may cause the same results. Of course, normally, the prospect of such a defeat is extremely remote if the Government's Party has a majority in the House, but the possibility is always in the background. Ordinarily, the Cabinet has great power over the House; it can fix nearly all the timetable; its Party Whips will make sure that there is a majority in every division in favour of the Government; it can, on suitable occasions, recommend a dissolution, and normally a dissolution is most unwelcome to members, for obvious reasons.

In the last resort, the Commons is politically supreme, and can, if a majority of its members so resolve, dismiss any government at any time. In issues of the greatest moment, it has done so in the past, and may doubtless do so again. But ordinarily, the efforts of His Majesty's Opposition do not result in the defeat of the Government. What those efforts do result in more or less all the time is the modification of the Government's actions. Both Government and Opposition must for all the time be bearing in mind the effect of present activities on votes at the next election; both sides are out to capture the 'floating votes' next time, and both must therefore be for ever playing the game of 'give-and-take'. No government in its senses will refuse facilities for a debate of no confidence; no government can for a moment afford to ignore that intangible but highly potent quality, 'the sense of the House', which is not wholly a matter of Party sense; it may often be rather a matter of common sense. The Government's sails are often trimmed to meet winds that may blow, or threaten to blow, from any quarter of the House.

The King in Parliament is legally sovereign. Parliament can make, amend, or repeal any law whatsoever. Its legislative power is unlimited and absolute. No Act of Parliament can be unconstitutional, for the law of the land knows not the word or the idea. No person or body can overrule the King in Parliament; only Parliament itself can repeal its Acts; it is not bound by its own Acts in the past, nor can it bind its successors. Otherwise, it is as free as any legislature can be. It is limited only by the limits to the willingness of the people to obey its enactments, and by the limits imposed by the limited capacities of its own members.

Parliament has a place in the polity far transcending its purely legal functions. It is the great forum of political opinion and debate. It is the place wherein H.M. Government can and does lead and also test opinion on matters of great and small moment, and of more than Party significance. It is the place wherein H.M. Opposition can and does influence policy. It can be, and sometimes is, a Council of State, the 'grand inquest' of the nation. On issues of great import the House may and often does speak to the world with one voice, and reveal the underlying unity of the nation, amid all its diversities and Party differences. When this happens, Parliament is more than a legislature; it is the expression of the profoundest convictions of a people.

His Majesty's Judges and H.M. Government

A detailed description of the Judiciary in a very short account of the English Constitution is not essential,[1] but some mention of the important place of the judges of the High Court in relation to acts of the Government is indispensable.

His Majesty's Judges enjoy a very special position in the State. Appointed by the Crown on the recommendation of the Government (i.e., in practice, of the Lord Chancellor), they are nevertheless as independent of the Government as it is possible to be. They hold office during good behaviour; their salaries are paid out of the Consolidated Fund and are not subject to annual parliamentary vote; they can be removed from office by the Crown on a petition from both Houses of Parliament, probably only by that method; they enjoy complete immunity in the exercise of their office; no action lies against a judge for any acts done or words spoken in his judicial capacity. Furthermore, the judges are invariably chosen from among men eminent at the Bar; they are therefore professional lawyers, and are in no sense civil servants, either by training, outlook, or status. This circumstance, determined by a most fortunate choice of our medieval kings, has been of the utmost importance in the development of both the law and the constitution.

The primary function of the judges is, of course, to determine disputes either between subject and subject, or between subject and State. They must apply the law of the land, and are bound to follow statutes and previous decisions of their own or superior courts. In the process they must necessarily interpret the law, and by their decisions make law. The common law of England is the great monument to centuries of judicial activity.

From the purely constitutional point of view, the function of the judges is to ensure that the executive does not exceed its powers as defined by law at any given time, in so far as such matters come before them in court. Upon them rests the practical responsibility for maintaining the rule of law. It is not for them to question the exercise by the Government of a lawful discretion; but it is for them to determine the legality of any act of the Government which is called in question in the court. It is not for them to nullify any act as being unconstitutional (as the judges of the

[1] It is all the less needful here, in view of the volume in this Series entitled *English Courts of Law*, by H. G. Hanbury (1944, 4th ed. prepared by D. C. M. Yardley, 1967).

Supreme Court in the United States may do); they are concerned only with the question whether legal authority, by prerogative, statute, or common law, exists for any power that has in fact been exercised and is disputed in court. This is a duty of the greatest importance, and is the bulwark of the liberties of the citizen.

The executive can only exercise powers which by law appertain to it; otherwise the courts will rule it *ultra vires*. Thus a Department might make an Order for which there is no statutory authority, or which exceeds the provisions of an Act, or is inconsistent with the Act by virtue of which it has been made.[1] If it does, and an aggrieved party brings the matter before the court, the Order will be nullified, and the Department will have to think again. Similarly, the courts will uphold the principles of natural justice, e.g. that no man shall be a judge in his own case, that both parties to a dispute ought to be heard, in cases where a Minister or Department has come to an apparently judicial decision in a manner alien to those principles.

The courts are not without powerful weapons with which to review the acts of the Government, and indeed of lesser authorities. They may issue prerogative writs or orders commanding that certain things shall be done or not done. Of these the most important and famous is the writ of *Habeas Corpus*, but the other writs (now Orders)[2] of *Mandamus*, *Prohibition*, and *Certiorari* are instruments of more frequent resort under modern conditions.

The writ of *Habeas Corpus* is the great and effective remedy to protect the individual from unlawful imprisonment and detention. Any imprisoned or detained person, or any person acting on his behalf, may apply for the writ to any judge of the High Court, who is bound, under heavy penalties, to issue the writ on prima-facie cause being shown. The procedure is simple and expeditious. On cause being shown, the judge, as a matter of course, issues a peremptory order to the detainer to appear and show cause why a writ of *Habeas Corpus* should not be issued against him. If on appearance and argument, the judge is satisfied that the application is sound, the writ is forthwith issued, requiring the production

[1] The decision of the House of Lords in *Minister of Health* v. *the King* (1931) lays down that even when the enabling statute gives power to make an Order, which when made 'shall have effect as if enacted in the Act', the Order made must be consistent with the Act itself if it is to be valid. Cf. above, p. 24.

[2] The Administration of Justice (Miscellaneous Provisions) Act, 1938, abolished the writs and substituted more modern Orders.

of the prisoner in court on an appointed day, whereupon he is released if no sufficient cause for detention is proved. If sufficient cause is proved, then a speedy trial is ensured, thus making it impossible for the executive to detain a person for an indefinite period. The writ is issuable to anyone, whether a Secretary of State, a Minister, military authority, or any person whatsoever. It is a highly effective remedy for unlawful detention, but it does not of itself provide damages or penalties for unlawful detention or assault, to obtain which separate proceedings are required and available.

There are times when it would not be in the national interest to restrict so rigidly the power of H.M. Government to arrest and detain persons suspected of treasonable activities or intentions, and in times of emergency the *Habeas Corpus* procedure has been partially suspended by Act of Parliament.[1] But such suspensions are only of the remedy in relation to persons suspected of particular offences, such as treason, and do not make lawful what is otherwise unlawful imprisonment.

The other procedures, of *Mandamus*, *Prohibition*, and *Certiorari*, enable the courts to exercise a certain degree of supervision over the executive (and other authorities), in the sense of requiring it (or them) to keep to the law. All three Orders issue from the King's Bench Division of the High Court.

Mandamus is a peremptory order commanding a body or a person to do its or his legal duty. It does not lie against the Crown, and therefore cannot be used to compel the performance of duties existing only by virtue of the royal prerogative, but can be, and is, used to oblige a Department to perform duties imposed upon it by statute. It can be, and is, issued to other bodies and persons on behalf of an applicant who has a right to the performance of a legal duty, if he has no other suitable means of compulsion. The Order is thus a valuable instrument for ensuring the performance of legal duties of all kinds other than those resting on prerogative.

The Order of *Prohibition* works in the opposite sense, and is used to forbid an excess of legal powers. It may be used to prevent a lower court from exceeding its jurisdiction or from acting contrary to the rules of natural justice; it may be issued against Ministers of the Crown, or public or semi-public bodies to control

[1] Suspension of the *Habeas Corpus* Act during the war of 1939–45 was not necessary, as wide powers of imprisonment without trial were conferred on the Secretary of State under Emergency Regulations.

the exercise of judicial or quasi-judicial functions. Its precise scope has never been defined, but its value as a means of preventing excess of jurisdiction or powers by courts or Ministers is not in doubt.

Certiorari issues to remove a suit from an inferior court into the High Court. It may be used to secure a fairer trial or to prevent an excess of jurisdiction, and may be issued before, during, or after a trial. It is applicable to review a judicial act in the widest sense, whether the act of an ordinary court of law or of a Minister, or of any authority engaged in a judicial capacity. The difference between *Prohibition* and *Certiorari* rests on the fact that the former restrains the recipient from proceeding further in the matter, whilst the latter requires the matter to be sent into the King's Bench for inquiry to be made as to its legality; but naturally the scope of the two procedures may overlap, and both may be appropriate.

Recent Acts of Parliament have tended to simplify and reduce the consequent cost of these procedures, to the benefit of the citizen. His Majesty's Judges thus remain, as in the past, in the proud position of guardians of the law of the realm, the instruments of the King's justice, charged with the duty of securing that His Majesty's Government and all other authorities and persons act within the law as it in fact exists at any given time.

His Majesty's Subjects and the Law of the Land

His Majesty's subjects possess no guarantees of freedom. The 'rights of man' are not guaranteed nor even mentioned anywhere in English constitutional law. There being no written documentary Constitution, no high-sounding declaration of the liberties of the individual exists. Various Constitutions have been promulgated in other countries which include the enunciation of noble principles of individual rights. But often these declarations have proved to be not worth the paper on which they are printed, for sometimes it is not difficult to bring about the suspension of written Constitutions, and of the 'guaranteed' liberties along with them.

His Majesty's subjects are in theory therefore in a disadvantageous position compared with the citizens who live under a written Constitution of this kind, but in practice they are far better off. The secret of English liberty rests on the fact that any subject is entirely free to do what he likes and to say what he likes, provided only that he does not thereby break the law as it exists at the time. If his freedoms are infringed, he has his remedies in the ordinary law of the land as enforced in the courts. He cannot be deprived of any of his liberties or of his remedies, except by Act of Parliament.

He is personally free, because detention is legally justifiable on only a very few well-defined grounds, e.g. on a criminal charge, whilst serving a sentence after conviction, on certifiable lunacy, by the exercise of parental (but not marital) authority. If he is detained on other than lawful grounds, he has his remedies: he may, in certain circumstances, resort to self-help and resist with violence; he may prosecute for assault, or take proceedings for wrongful arrest (against the police as well as other persons); he may obtain a writ of *Habeas Corpus* against his detainer.

He enjoys freedom of property, within the limits of the law. Trespass or conversion of property are civil wrongs, and if malicious may be criminal also. If the citizen's property is disturbed or invaded by other than lawfully constituted authority, he has his remedies in the courts.

He is free to say what he likes about anything or anybody, and can make the rudest remarks about His Majesty's Government, subject simply to the existing laws of defamation (slander and libel), and to the very rarely invoked laws relating to blasphemy, obscenity, sedition, and incitement to mutiny.

His right to hold public meetings is merely the right of individuals to do and say what they like, subject to the general law of the land. It is a statutory offence to prevent the transaction of business at a lawful public meeting, and a public meeting is unlawful only if it seeks to effect a purpose which would be unlawful for an individual to effect, except that conspiracy of two or more persons to effect an unlawful purpose is an aggravation and is in itself a criminal offence.

A public meeting may trespass, commit a nuisance, or utter defamatory words, and consequently its participants may be liable under the law relating to those offences, and if a breach of the peace is apprehended, the meeting is an unlawful assembly and can be lawfully dispersed, and its participants are guilty of a misdemeanour. If an unlawful assembly takes some actual step towards achieving its purpose, it degenerates into a rout, and may incur heavier penalties. If it actually puts an unlawful purpose into effect, it becomes a riot, a misdemeanour punishable by imprisonment, and if the unlawful purpose is itself a felony, e.g. arson, the riot is felonious, and incurs still heavier penalties, and the force used to disperse it may be greater. Continued participation in a riot becomes in itself felonious, if the assembly fails to disperse within one hour after a magistrate has read the proclamation under the Riot Act of 1714, and thereby ordered twelve or more persons assembled together to the disturbance of the public peace to disperse.

The freedoms of the individual thus remain extensive, and are practically unlimited in respect of the expression of political and religious opinion. Minorities are free to become majorities, by persuasion, if they can. Freedom of this kind is the life-blood of the Constitution. By it the Constitution has grown and become what it is, and could not survive without its perpetually re-invigorating stream.

His Majesty's subjects have duties as well as rights. It is the duty of every citizen to assist in quelling disorder, if called upon to do so by any lawfully constituted authority, e.g. a police constable.

Every subject owes allegiance to the Crown, and so does every alien, other than an enemy alien interned as a civilian or confined as a prisoner of war, whilst resident in His Majesty's domains. Breach of allegiance is treason, and punishable by death. It is treason to compass or imagine the death of the King, or Queen, or the King's eldest son and heir, if accompanied by an overt act; or to encompass bodily harm or imprisonment to the King; it is treason to levy war against the King within the realm, or to adhere to the King's enemies, giving them aid or comfort within the realm or elsewhere.[1] It is misprision of treason to fail to report treason to a properly constituted authority, and it is treason-felony to compass or devise to depose the King, or to levy war to make him change his counsels or to overawe either House of Parliament, or to incite foreigners to invade the realm or any of His Majesty's domains, in either case punishable by imprisonment.

His Majesty's subjects enjoy great privileges, and are fortunate among mankind, the great bulk of whom are in a very different position. It is fitting that the betrayer of his duty, the traitor, or, by ancient usage, the *perfidus*, should render account and pay his forfeit.

[1] The law of treason was in effect strengthened in certain particulars by the Treachery Act of 1940.

2
The Medieval Foundations

THE MOST FUNDAMENTAL INSTITUTIONS and many of the basic assumptions of the English Constitution are very ancient, and are medieval in origin. The monarchy spans the whole of English history; the principal institutions of central government, including parliament, were both royal and medieval in origination; the basic notions of the duty of the subjects to participate in government, and of the overriding supremacy of the law, if not exactly royal in origin, were characteristic features of the medieval polity from a very early date.

The contributions of modern times to the Constitution have in the main taken the form of building on medieval foundations, and of modifying the relations between various parts of those foundations, rather than of original creation. Naturally, these modern developments have altered the actual scheme of government almost out of recognition. It could be argued that the constitutional history of England is essentially a sequence of different Constitutions rather than one continuous history. There would be truth in such an argument, but the fact is that each of those historic Constitutions has merged imperceptibly into the one following, and the difficulty would be to determine at what point to draw the line between the periods in the sequence. All historical periods flow into each other in a remorseless stream, defying and frustrating the neat classifications and generalizations of historians. Much of the past is ever-present; which is the same thing as saying that much of what seems to be modern is really medieval. In Western Europe, the Middle Ages were by far the most creative of all ages in the art of government; for they created the basis of modern government out of primeval anarchy. The modern ages have in fact created little; but they have adapted much.

English constitutional history, for all practical purposes, begins with the Anglo-Saxon and Jutish settlements in England in the fifth and sixth centuries A.D. Needless to say, the island had been inhabited by human beings for many thousands of years before that, but no one has succeeded in showing that the immensely long history of the Stone-Age men, or of the aboriginal Britons, or the four hundred years of Roman Britain had any permanent effect, or indeed any effect at all upon the course of English history in the governmental or constitutional sphere. Naturally, in some highly important respects, in the composition of the population above all, and possibly in some aspects of rural economy, topography, and the like, the remote past has its effects upon all subsequent history, but matters of this kind do not concern us in this discussion.

It is true that the Jutes and Anglo-Saxons who settled in what later came to be known as England did not drop down from heaven upon the place beneath. They had had a long history behind them, and some sort of governmental arrangements of a tribal variety in those parts of NW. Germany from which they migrated, and it cannot be doubted that that history profoundly affected all the later history of England. The difficulty is that we know next to nothing of that history. What we do know of it comes mainly from the brief, alien, and none too reliable accounts written up for their own good purposes by Julius Caesar and by Tacitus five hundred and three hundred and fifty years respectively before the settlement. For practical purposes, therefore, English Constitutional History, as a subject for study, although not in reality, begins with the Anglo-Saxons and Jutes after the settlement, and it begins in England.

The Origins of Central Government

The foundations of central government in England were laid during the medieval period, well before the end of the fifteenth century. Modern constitutional history is taken up with little more than changes in the balance of powers and principles among and within the fundamental institutions of national government created during the thousand years that elapsed from the time of the settlement of the English until the end of what are usually called the Middle Ages.

The great task of creating the foundations of central government out of a confused welter of local diversities, a task fundamental to all subsequent constitutional development, and indeed to the existence and survival of the nation itself, was the immortal achievement of the medieval monarchy. The impelling motive of the most constructive of these kings was, of course, primarily to strengthen the power of the Crown, and, partly as a result, to secure better governance for their realm. The task was not easy to accomplish; the beginnings of royal power were rather feeble, and the resources and opportunities open to the Crown were for a long time very limited. In the earlier medieval period, up to the middle of the thirteenth century, the monarchy had to contend not so much with conscious political opposition as with the force of unpropitious circumstances and the conservatism of ancient custom. The early medieval period did not provide an environment in which centralized government could readily flourish. The forces of tribalism and localism in general were very old and powerful, and died hard. Local custom, local power, and local ambitions of all kinds formed the natural obstacles and materials with which the monarchy had to contend, and there was no centralizing impulse anywhere except that emanating from the Crown, and in some degree from the Church, mainly but not exclusively in ecclesiastical affairs.

It was during the course of the thirteenth century, in the reign of Henry III, that the Crown, almost for the first time, had to contend with a different kind of difficulty, the difficulty of conscious political opposition. This opposition came from the only class in the community capable of any political initiative at that time—from the ranks of the greater feudal baronage, who were by law and custom vested with vast estates and important governmental rights over the inhabitants of those estates. But the extraordinary and indeed crucial fact about this nascent political opposition was that the baronage who opposed the king's will had at no time the intention of destroying or even of seriously modifying the structure of the central government as such and of grasping at independent power for themselves. By then the institutions of central government were too well founded for that; the creative efforts of some of the Anglo-Saxon kings, and of such great rulers as William the Conqueror, Henry I, and Henry II, and their ministers, were not to be in vain. So far from wanting to destroy central government, the baronial opposition of the thirteenth century strove to control it, and to oblige the king to pursue policies agreeable to them. All subsequent constitutional struggles, from that day to this, have been over the control and exercise of the powers of the central government, not over the fundamentals of its existence. England consequently escaped the unhappy experiences of some continental countries, in which at times the very survival of central government itself was imperilled.

The polities which emerged from the Jutish and Anglo-Saxon settlements in the later fifth and early sixth centuries were kingdoms, and early English history centred around the kingships. By the end of the sixth century at least ten separate kingdoms had come into existence, and for some four hundred years the main theme in political history was the struggle for supremacy among these, or among the surviving, kingdoms. The creation of a unified kingdom was a slow and arduous process, partly impeded, but in the end assisted, by the conquest of the eastern and north-eastern parts of the country by the Danes, and also assisted in some degree, after the Conversion, by the Church, the outlook and aspirations of which were necessarily national rather than tribal. The struggle between Northumbria and Mercia in the seventh century led to the supremacy of Mercia under King Offa (757–96) in the latter half of the eighth century. The next century saw the rise of Wessex to paramountcy, and King Egbert of that House (802–39) had some claims to a general overlordship of England. The threat of a complete overrunning of the country by the Danes, which developed in the later ninth century, was checked by King Alfred (871–99) the greatest of Anglo-Saxon kings, who emerged as the national leader and hero of the English. In the tenth century the able rulers of the House of Wessex became in effect kings of the English part of the country, and substantial progress was made with the absorption of the Danish regions (Danelagh) into the framework of the administrative system, although many parts of that area, especially the more northern, retained their own Danish legal customs for a long time to come. But the completion of this great task was prevented by the renewal of invasion on a powerful scale from Scandinavia, and the virtual conquest of the whole country by Sweyn and Cnut in the early eleventh century. Political unification came not from the House of Wessex, but from the Danes, and Cnut (1017–35) was enabled to style himself king of all England, and to rule with wisdom and ability over a formally unified kingdom.

Cnut, in the early eleventh century, like William the Conqueror half a century later, displayed statesmanlike qualities of a high order, and neither of the two conquerors sought to destroy the traditions and status built up by their predecessors in the kingship. On the contrary, both regarded themselves as the heirs of the House of Wessex, and inheritors of whatever prestige and powers were enjoyed by the old kings. So it came about that there was no break, despite two conquests, in the continuity of the monarchy, and the traditions of the Anglo-Saxon kingship became permanently woven into the texture of the English monarchy.

The old Anglo-Saxon monarchy was an institution very different indeed from the immensely powerful, dominant monarchy of the central Middle Ages, and from any modern conception of kingship. The early Anglo-Saxon kings were not supported by any extensive legal rights nor armed with any very powerful weapons for enforcing government. They were more potent in the moral than in the material sphere. The kings headed the nation, embodied the tribal consciousness, and constituted living symbols of religious and even mystical significance in the eyes of their people, at first in a purely pagan, and later in a more Christian, sense. They were venerated as descendants of the ancient deities, but after the Conversion, the possibility and progress of which depended in the early days entirely upon royal favour, and after the general alliance between monarchy and the Church (which has lasted with intermissions and in different forms to this day), they received the blessing and the invaluable support of the Church. By the eighth century, the descendants of Woden had become kings 'by the grace of God', and were crowned and anointed by the Church, and took a coronation oath of great importance as emphasizing the moral obligations of the kingship. In origin, the kings must have been little more than the successful leaders of fighting immigrants, but from a very early date the duties of kingship became idealized. The king was regarded as having the duties of defending his people, of upholding the law, and of doing justice. The office of king, possibly purely elective in the earliest times, became hereditary within the royal family, although an elective element remained, enabling a choice to be made between suitable and less suitable candidates from among the members of the family.

The old English king was not the source of law, even though it was his duty to enforce it as far as he could—which was often not very far. Law was tribal custom, or folkright, to which the king was subordinate in every respect, as any other member of the folk.

He might, and on occasion did, find it necessary to declare, with the express or tacit assent of some of the 'wise men' of his realm (the *witan*), what the law was on certain points, and even to commit such declarations to writing. Several of the kings, from the time of Ethelbert of Kent (*c.* 601–4), promulgated laws (*dooms*) which have survived, but there was very little law-making in a formal sense in the early Middle Ages, and it is very doubtful whether the notion of legislation existed at all. Certainly the king was not regarded in any sense as an arbitrary law-giver. The law was essentially impersonal in origin, and resided in ancient custom and the communal mind of the folk. The courts of law were not as yet the king's courts, but were folkmoots in which the law was pronounced and judgements reached, not by royal judges or officials, but by the freemen of the vicinity acting as the suitors or doomsmen of the moot. The king's part was but to try to enforce the law and judgements of the moots, to use such poor resources as he had on the side of justice, and to suppress violence too great for others to deal with.

The basic concept of Anglo-Saxon law, derived from very ancient Germanic custom, was that of the rights of the freeman, as enshrined in the law of the folk (folkright). Social inequality was the rule from the very earliest times for which we have any evidence. The freemen were not all equal in status, and in most regions, especially in the more southern, a nobility by birth existed; below the freemen in the social scale came semi-freemen, and even slaves or rightless men. But the characteristic which proved to be of permanent and fundamental importance in history was the strong position accorded by immemorial custom to the common free man, the lawful man, as he came to be called in later times. That position might deteriorate, and did so in the later Anglo-Saxon period, when the freeman class became depressed by the force of political and economic circumstances. Many men in the eleventh century, whose ancestors had been fully free within the limits of ancient custom, found themselves in a position, not of freedom, but of serfdom, bound to the land and bound to perform arduous labour services on the land of a lord to whom they must needs look for protection and the means of livelihood. But the growth of villeinage or serfdom in the later Anglo-Saxon period, to be continued after the Norman Conquest, never destroyed the concept of the rights and duties of the freeman, the notion of the law-worthy or lawful man, fit for the responsibilities and duties of what we should call citizenship, able and willing to co-operate in the manifold and ever-growing tasks of good government. The king's government was to find it very useful to place many arduous duties upon the lawful men, and indeed only with their assistance was it possible for the Crown to make a government work at all. In time it was from this class, or at least from sections of it, that the Crown was to exact much responsibility in the administration of justice; in time representatives of it were to be summoned to participate in the government at the centre, to meet the king's council in parliament. That was in the distant future, but the fundamental assumption of the trustworthiness of the lawful free man was Anglo-Saxon in origin, and was part and parcel of ancient Germanic custom.

In the earliest times the rights of the freeman were closely bound up with the notion of kindred, of the blood-tie as the fundamental bond between men, and therefore as the basis of legal rights and duties. Very likely the earliest social and therefore political units were kins; the earliest form of criminal-law enforcement was certainly based upon the principles of blood-feud, and crimes against the person were matters for settlement between the kindred concerned. It was to his kin that a man looked for the support and testimony required by custom to make him reputable and law-worthy in the folkmoots. How far these notions were carried in early Anglo-Saxon times is still the subject of much learned controversy. That they were not carried to their logical conclusion, and that they were not at any time after the settlement the only notions operative in the early kingdoms, seems to be certain. The undoubted existence of monarchy from the earliest days of written record—and indeed earlier—must have had some modifying effect upon any aboriginal society based simply upon kinship, and from quite an early date we know that social and legal bonds other than the ties of kindred were operative. The startling phenomenon of churchmen with no kin or tie was something undreamt of in the folkright of pagan times, and it is significant that the first clause of the earliest known royal declaration of law (by Ethelbert of Kent, *c.* 601–4) attempts to fit the clergy into the scheme of customary rights. Furthermore, as time went on, many men who for one reason or another moved away from their original environments and sought their fortunes elsewhere, in the service of greater men, or the king, or otherwise, could not depend on ties of kindred to make them law-worthy and reputable. But for the purposes of law and order it was essential that every freeman should have somebody to support him and to swear for him in court if the need arose, and to be responsible for his good behaviour, and so it came about that such men were required, sometimes by royal ordinance, to find someone of good repute and respectability to stand towards them and to act for them in law as if they were of their kin. In this, and other ways, the relationship of lord and man came into being, and it was to flourish considerably in the centuries to follow. Moreover, as time passed, the basic tie of kinship receded into the background, and legal and social bonds became territorialized. A man's neighbours came to take the place of kindred in a number of ways. The lawful men of the neighbourhood came to be charged with many legal responsibilities and duties, and the time was to come, after the Norman Conquest, when the sworn testimony of the neighbourhood, the verdict of the countryside, would be of the utmost importance not only in the administration of justice, but in the carrying out of the king's government in the country generally.

During the century or so before the Norman Conquest, the old English monarchy did succeed in making a good deal of progress towards the better realization of the ideals of governance, which then meant little beyond the better enforcement of law and order. The way was long and arduous, for violence on all sides was habitual, the difficulties of suppressing it very great. But the monarchy succeeded to by William the Conqueror in 1066 was a very much more effective institution than it had been in the earlier days, even though Edward the Confessor himself attained no great distinction or success as a ruler, and Harold, the last of the old English kings, had no time vouchsafed to him to carry on the traditions.

The remarkable process whereby the great departments of state were evolved out of the king's own Household began long before the Norman Conquest. If central institutions of government were to develop at all, there was indeed no source from which they could have sprung, except from among the king's intimates and servants of his Household, from the king's permanent court. The process of development was a very slow one, impelled only by the gradual expansion of the powers and scope of royal government, and by the growing need for the king to be assisted in the tasks of government by reliable men who could understand what they were doing and who would seek above all to carry out the king's will. The origins of the executive and of the civil service (the two were of course indistinguishable until notions of ministerial responsibility to someone other than the king developed in the seventeenth century) are to be found in the Households of the Anglo-Saxon kings.

That this process must have gone far long before the Norman Conquest cannot be doubted, for no king could have discharged even the modest functions expected of him in those days without the aid of intimates and servants, especially if he himself, like nearly all his lay contemporaries, could neither read nor write. He could call upon the counsel of his *witan*, the wise and great men of his realm, to assist him in deciding matters of great moment and in formulating policy, but this could only be on occasions and at long intervals. The daily tasks of government could not wait upon periodical assemblies of the wise and the great in those days, any more than they can now. The king must needs rely extensively upon the intimates and servants who were always with him. We do not know very much about the processes or organization of the centre of the king's government in the Anglo-Saxon period. It is, however, certain that the rudiments, and indeed more than the rudiments, of a secretariat existed in the royal Household long before the Norman Conquest. The clerics who had a place in the king's hall, and wrote up a long stream of royal charters and writs, at first in the vernacular, later and more usually in Latin, supervised by an officer who, even though not called the Chancellor before the Conquest, certainly was soon after it, were the prototypes of His Majesty's civil servants. The nucleus of the future Chancery certainly existed before the Norman Conquest, and used a king's seal (later to be the Great Seal) to authenticate its documents. Other domestic officials, such as the chamberlains of the king's Bedchamber, in which the royal treasures and cash were habitually kept, were laying the foundations of another department destined to have a great future before it—the Treasury.

It was also very necessary for the king to procure reliable links between himself and the localities far and wide; otherwise no royal government could make itself felt in the country at large. The king acquired these links by creating in effect a new class in the community, the class known as *thegns*, who eventually came to be, in their higher ranks at least, a new nobility, not by blood, but by virtue of office and service to the king, and who in time, in consequence of being rewarded for service by the grant of lands, became a landed, but hardly an hereditary, aristocracy. In origin the king's men, these *thegns* tended to become local magnates. But, by and large, from the eighth century at least, the king was well served by this class of servant, not only at the centre, in all kinds of duties in his court, but also in the localities. Through them the king kept in constant touch with local affairs; through them the royal commands were communicated to royal officers resident in the shires; they delivered the king's charters and writs, and acted generally as the agents of the king's will to enforce law and order over the kingdom.

By these and other means the later Anglo-Saxon monarchs were able to engage in a great deal of administrative activity, directed mainly to the ever-present problems of law-enforcement. Moreover, the framework of local administration, which remained the essential structure of government throughout the Middle Ages, in some degree for much longer, and in part up to the present day, came into being. The units of the shire and hundred, basic for administrative, fiscal, and judicial purposes for many centuries, were Anglo-Saxon in origin and, in part at least, of royal creation, and if not of royal creation, came to be used to the full by the Crown for government purposes. The question of the origins of the shire and hundred (and their respective courts) is too complicated to pursue here, but the vital thing was that long before the Norman Conquest the Crown had learnt to use the shire and shire court, the hundred and hundred court, and the still smaller unit of the vill (roughly the village community) for many purposes of government, law-enforcement, and justice. Through these channels the royal will could in some degree be made effective far and wide.

But naturally the king's will could be applied only within the narrow spheres delimited for him by law and custom, and although law and custom might, and did, change, it was a slow process. The king's sphere of action was primarily to maintain the law, not to alter it (and, of course, to defend his people). There was still little or no idea of law-giving or legislation. Law might occasionally be declared (and doubtless be modified in the process) by the king, with the express or tacit assent of the wise men, but there was very little even of this in the later Anglo-Saxon period. There are, however, signs that the king did acquire a larger place in the scheme of law and justice during this period. He did, for example, get a hold over what was then the most powerful available weapon for law-enforcement—the procedure of outlawry, whereby a man was cast out of the protection of the law, and exposed to the tender mercies of anyone's man-hunt. It was a fearsome and brutal means of encouraging respect for the law among a mostly brutal and violent folk, and might be used for political as well as judicial ends. Cnut acquired the sole right of inlawing outlaws.

Further, the effective powers of the king to command obedience were enhanced in the tenth century by the development of recognized pecuniary penalties for failure to obey the king's express order or ban. By these and other means the king gained a greater effectiveness, and also greater responsibility for the enforcement of law and order, and more and more it was to the king's authority rather than to that of the ancient folkmoots that the people tended to look for enforcing justice. The origins of the notion of the king's peace are obscure and controversial, but that the notion had its influence before the Anglo-Saxon period was over cannot be doubted, and it was to have a great future before it. The first beginnings appeared of the idea that crime might be an offence against the king, rather than a mere private wrong. In short, the seeds of the mighty growth of the king's justice, in time to absorb all other sources of justice, were already sown.

The powers and the rudiments of central government to which the Norman kings succeeded were thus far from insignificant, and they brought with them the added prestige and potentialities of conquerors, as well as the standing and legal position of feudal overlords; above all, they brought also a tenacious will and an immense zest and ambition for power. Moreover, William the Conqueror and some at least of his successors displayed in a remarkable degree qualities of statesmanship and administrative ability.

The period from the Conquest to the death of Henry II (1189), if not indeed to that of Richard I (1199), can in some measure be regarded as a distinct and continuous phase in constitutional development, interrupted only by the usurpation and temporary breakdown of effective royal government during the time of Stephen (1135–54). This phase went far to determine that a strong and efficacious, and ever-expanding, royal government was going to be maintained, and that royal justice was going in the long run to triumph over all rival secular jurisdictions. By the end of Henry II's reign the foundations of central government had been so firmly laid that thereafter they were never seriously shaken.

This result was achieved by the Crown and its able servants, with the co-operation of many men who did not wish, or did not dare, to disobey the king's commands, and was achieved despite the, in some respects, unfavourable environment offered by the general feudalization of the community after the Norman Conquest.

Generalizations about feudalism (like most generalizations) are always false in some degree, because the 'feudal system' was essentially an unsystematic agglomeration of particular and diverse contracts and local customs, primarily concerned with individual rights of land tenure, which would not be of any great interest to constitutional historians at all, if it were not for the circumstance that certain, or rather uncertain, governmental rights and duties were inextricably bound up with feudal land tenure, and determined part of the conditions under which the monarchy fought its way to an overmastering Crown.

The essence of the whole 'system' was the principle of the hereditary tenure of land upon conditions of service of one kind or another. This was a principle which was not apparent in Anglo-Saxon society, and it is a mistake to suppose that genuine feudalism existed in England before the Norman Conquest. The notions of feudal contract and its many implications were imported by the Norman Conquerors, who had been familiar with such ideas and customs in the duchy of Normandy, and indeed they were common to Western Europe at the time. It is true that some features of Anglo-Saxon society at the time of the Conquest must have seemed to the Normans to be rather barbarous and vague imitations of their own more mature and precise conceptions of how things should be done, but none the less the structure of society was radically changed soon after the Conquest. The Conqueror assumed all the land to be forfeit, and regarded himself as being in a position to grant rights over any part of it not retained in his own hands—on conditions. No Anglo-Saxon king had considered himself to be in such a position.

Broadly speaking, in due course after the Conquest most of the land came to be parcelled out, in large or small pieces, to grantees in perpetual hereditary succession on conditions of service. These conditions were of different kinds, carrying different implications, and of varying degrees of respectability and importance. Conditions ranging from the purely honorific to the menial were devised; the Church might be granted tenure on the spiritual conditions of prayer for the soul of the grantor. But the most important among conditions of tenure was military service. The Conqueror granted to his principal supporters and companions in conquest large areas of land on condition that they brought him a specified number of knights duly equipped for military operations when required to do so. These grantees, holding their lands directly of the king as their overlord, the king's vassals or tenants-in-chief, whether laymen or ecclesiastics, inevitably contained within their ranks the great and powerful men of the realm, the men with whom the king had to reckon in his counsels, whose support or opposition might make all the difference between the practicable and the impracticable in government. No other class of laymen could dare to resist the king's will.

The tenants-in-chief, in order to be able to produce their quota of knights and to provide for the cultivation of the lands which they proposed to retain in their own hands for their own maintenance, naturally in their turn granted out rights to parts of their holding to other men (sub-tenants or sub-vassals) who then held of them on conditions; some on condition of military service when required, others on condition of various 'civilian' services; many of these sub-tenants would find it necessary to repeat the process and create further holdings from themselves. At the bottom of the scale, wherein the bulk of the population eventually found themselves, too low in the scheme of things to be the subjects of formal contracts or grants, came the serfs, the unfree, who for one reason or another found themselves dependent on the freemen, great or small, who, in return for labour services on their own domains, would provide them with a hovel, the use of a bit of land for their support, and the rudiments of subsistence.

Many of the rights and duties which the moderns regard as being public and governmental in character were regarded in the feudal age as appertinent to land tenure, and therefore as part of the private rights and duties acquired by individual tenants by virtue merely of tenure. The feudal contract between lord and vassal implied more than simply occasional knight service. It implied also the duty of giving counsel to the lord; of paying suit at, and sharing in the judgements of, the lord's court held for the adjudication of disputes among vassals in the light of feudal law and custom; of giving him financial aid on certain customary occasions and at other times in case of need; of paying him homage and swearing fealty to him, as well as implying various other obligations. An extensive network of mutual obligations and duties spread over and penetrated all or nearly all branches of society, and this far-reaching scheme of contractual relationships, apart altogether from the intrinsic rules and customs, necessarily had a profound influence upon, and set part at least of the stage for, all subsequent constitutional development. Society, in spite of much diversity of custom in detail, became decidedly more closely knit than it had ever been in the past; the ties and mutual obligations between men became more clearly apparent and more capable of legal definition. On the one hand, a strong element of contractual and therefore mutual obligation entered into men's ideas of government; and, on the other hand, a further tincture of legalism was added to mental attitudes in general. Both features were to be of permanent importance.

It is often supposed that feudalization meant a weakening and hampering of the growth of central government. It is true that feudalism can only emerge where central government is weak—too weak to afford an adequate degree of protection and support to the individual in his struggle for existence and security—and that feudalism in one form or another always does develop where such conditions occur. Where central government is insufficiently effective to give protection against lawlessness and rapine, the ordinary folk will always gravitate around men who, for whatever reason, are in fact able to exercise a local power and to offer some protection from the wrong-doings of others. All that the ordinary person has to offer to the powerful individual in exchange for protection is personal service of one kind or another. A relationship of lord and man is set up, and mutual obligations are entered into. The phenomenon is natural and inevitable in the circumstances, and although it is a sign of weakness in the central government, it is not necessarily hostile to its existence and further development. On the contrary, it may, as being the only possible alternative to utter chaos and anarchy, provide the essential breathing space, and preserve the rudiments of law and social organization, without which the central government could not retain its foothold. On the other hand, in a feudal age the power and ambitions of the local magnates may become so great and so overweening that the national government is strangled, and unable to maintain itself and find means for expansion.

In England it was the former rather than the latter of these possibilities that was realized in practice; on the Continent generally it was the latter rather than the former. In England the organic growth of the central royal power never became stifled by the alternative power of the great feudatory magnates. There were, indeed, times when the story might have had a different ending, but in the main the growth of royal power was continuous, with the result that it was not central government but feudalism itself which disappeared, at a date much earlier than it did in many countries in Europe. The unhappy consequences of this disparity of development are still with us, and no one can tell whether some of these consequences ever will be effaced.

In a sense, the rights and duties acquired by William the Conqueror and his successors in their capacities as feudal overlords represented an important supplementation of those they inherited from the Anglo-Saxon kingship. From the Conquest the monarchs were not only kings of the English, but also heads of the feudal hierarchy, the universal landlords, to whom many important duties were unquestionably owed by the greatest and most powerful men in the realm. The consequent duality in the position of the monarchy coloured and conditioned the course of history for at least four hundred years. The monarchy had two strings to its bow, and could use the one to strengthen the other, according to circumstances.

The monarchy, in spite of the, in some respects, hampering effects of feudal custom, serious departures from which might, and on occasion did, evoke violent but not necessarily unlawful resistance, got a good deal out of feudalism to strengthen its hands. The possibility of turning feudal forces to the advantage rather than to the disadvantage of the Crown was assured by the circumstance that in England (always the least theoretically-minded of countries) feudal conceptions were never pushed to their logical conclusions.

The Anglo-Norman kings, in addition to obtaining the revenues of the great estates which they retained in their own hands, got many advantages out of feudalism. They got the counsel of their tenants-in-chief, an army, all kinds of services, important pecuniary and other profits, and they got, through homage and fealty, a direct tie with the most important, and, in time, with many less important, men of the realm.

Just as any feudal lord or baron had the right to the counsel of his sub-vassals, so the king could call upon the advice and secure the assent of his tenants-in-chief. He could summon whom he would from among his tenants-in-chief, great or small, to meet him—and such of his officials as he might select—to discuss the affairs of the realm, to commit them in advance to policy, to participate with him in judicial decisions, and if necessary to share in declarations of law. In time the greater men came to assert a right to do these things, and thereby to exert pressure upon the king. But in the early days service of this kind was a duty rather than a right. The periodic meetings of the king with his tenants-in-chief constituted enlargements of the king's permanent court, the *Curia Regis* of the eleventh and twelfth centuries, at its most solemn and impressive level; meetings of this kind came to be known as great councils in the thirteenth century, and these were to be the nuclei of the future parliaments, and the direct ancestors of the House of Lords.

The provision of an army of knights was the *raison d'être* of tenure by military service. The army so provided was not perhaps a very mobile or very numerous force (probably the maximum number of knights obtainable through it never exceeded five thousand); it was difficult to employ for more than the customary forty days at a time, and of doubtful utility for service abroad. But once mobilized, it did provide for the king's use a force greater than anything likely to be put into the field against him, at any rate within the realm. Nor was military service the only tenure useful to the king in his royal capacity. All sorts of services could be and were got from other conditions of tenure; services honorific, domestic, and menial; arms and munitions of war were supplied to the king as conditions of tenure.

From the lands retained in his own hands, the royal demesne lands, the king obtained substantial hereditary revenues, out of which he was expected to meet the expenses of government generally, but which were, of course, outside any control and independent of anyone's grant; herein lay one of the most important reasons why it was to prove so difficult to impose any enduring control over the king's government later on; the later parliament could not exercise any effective power of the purse until the time came when the hereditary revenues of the Crown no longer sufficed for the ordinary, as distinct from the extraordinary, expenses of government. In addition, the feudal king got financial aids from his tenants-in-chief, and could recover lands previously granted out in the event of the grantee's having no heirs, or of treason or felony committed by the grantee. The ceremonies of homage and fealty provided a legal and moral bond between the king and his tenants, and in time the oath of fealty came to be exacted from others than tenants-in-chief, and closer ties were knit between king and subjects.

Feudal conceptions were not, in England, ever carried to the extreme. The king's court was never completely feudalized; the king could summon to it whom he would, and in time—and in a sense—he could and did summon to it knights of the shire and burgesses of the cities and boroughs regardless of tenurial questions, and by force of royal command alone. Judicature was never confined to feudal courts: the old communal courts of shire and hundred continued to function, and were to provide a stepping-stone for a vast expansion of royal justice. The raising of revenue was never restricted merely to feudal aids, even though the need for consent to feudal aids other than customary ones is the origin of modern principles of taxation. The retention of the old direct tax on land—the Danegeld originally imposed before the Conquest as a means of buying off the Danes—kept the door open for the occasional imposition of non-feudal, national taxation, which by the end of the twelfth century came to be levied on movables rather than on land. The homage paid by sub-vassals to their lords always reserved fidelity to the king; no one was bound to fight for his lord against the lord king. Nor was knight service the only source of military support upon which the king could rely in the hour of need. In Anglo-Saxon times the duty of bearing arms had been obligatory upon all freemen; service in the national militia (*fyrd*) was not abolished by the Conqueror; on the contrary, it was preserved, and was better defined and brought up to date by his successors. This remarkable piece of statesmanship served the monarchy well; the king could and on occasion did mobilize the national militia against invaders and, above all, against refractory feudal barons. The militia was a trump card in the hands of the monarchy.

In short, feudalism did not present insuperable obstacles to the expansion of royal and central government. Within fifty years of the Conquest, during the reign of Henry I (1100–35), a constructive period, an era of distinct progress in government, set in. Not very much evidence of it survives, for his reign was followed by that of Stephen, during which the Crown was temporarily overshadowed by civil war and by the disintegrating influences of feudal anarchy at its worst. But there is good reason to suppose that much of the permanently important development during the great reign of Henry II (1154–89) had been anticipated under his grandfather, Henry I.

The work of Henry II and his advisers proved in the long run to be decisive. Not only were the institutions of central government much improved, but, in addition, ways and means had been found for a vast and steady increase in the power of the Crown in the sphere always fundamental to good government, and then as now of paramount urgency and interest to the people at large—the sphere of justice.

By 1189, the development of departments and officers 'of state' from out of the Household had been carried very much further. The Chancery and the Exchequer had acquired a clear identity and distinct functions of their own. The Chancery was the royal secretariat with a multitude of duties, and its head, the Chancellor, had become an officer of high status and dignity (often rewarded for his services by being given a bishopric through royal influence), and, although emphatically the king's servant, was gradually acquiring the standing of a great officer of state, of semi-ministerial quality. The Exchequer had become a regular, well-organized financial department, with a mature and elaborate system of financial administration and audit, revealed in detail in the first treatise on public administration, the famous *Dialogue Concerning the Exchequer*, written by one of the department's creators, about 1177. In the Chancery and the Exchequer Henry II and his successors possessed highly skilled instruments of government.

Out of the judicial work carried on by the *Curia* were to evolve more specialized judicial functions, and eventually courts of judicature. The financial side was to retain the name 'Exchequer', but the legal side, which inevitably included pleas between subject and subject as well as pleas concerning the royal interests, was soon to be called the Bench, or Common Bench, and so far as pleas between subject and subject were concerned, was to throw off a jurisdiction which in the thirteenth century was to develop a separate existence as the Court of Common Pleas. Other judicial matters, especially those of particular difficulty or of special interest to the King, continued to be dealt with by members of the general *Curia*, actually or theoretically *coram rege* (in the presence of the King). From this source the separate court of King's Bench was destined to develop in the later thirteenth century, whilst the Exchequer of Pleas maintained its jurisdiction in royal financial and cognate causes. Moreover, Henry II carried much further a practice occasionally adopted by some of his predecessors by more frequently and regularly sending out justices from his *Curia* to hold in effect local sessions of the king's court in the shire court. These justices itinerant started the circuits of royal justice which have been carried on, with little intermission, from that day to this.

The monarchy, it might be said, had entered into active competition with many old-established rivals for the supply of a desirable commodity in great demand—justice. For in the localities there were many different purveyors of justice, who, in the main, had hitherto sufficed for the dispensation of both criminal and civil justice. The old communal courts of shire and hundred were still exercising their ancient criminal and other customary jurisdictions; hundredal jurisdiction, as well as other species of judicature, had often come to be vested in private hands, in theory by specific royal grant, even long before the Norman Conquest; every feudal lord, by virtue of tenure, had a court for the settlement of feudal disputes among his tenants, and every lord of a manor—and in theory there was scarcely any part of the land not comprised within a manor—applied the custom of the manor in his manorial court.

There was little possibility, therefore, of royal justice making much headway amid this forest of jurisdictions, unless it could provide litigants with a better and more acceptable article than could be got elsewhere. But the Crown did succeed in doing so, and did it largely by creating a far better judicial procedure and by ensuring a more manifest justice than any of its rivals could do. The time was to come when royal justice would monopolize the market.

The most important of the procedures introduced by the Crown was the sworn inquest of lawful men, the jury. Reliance upon the sworn testimony of the neighbourhood was not new at this time; there was a long history behind it. Possibly it was derived from the Romans through the Franks, and it had been resorted to for certain purposes by the Norman kings. The famous Domesday Book survey of the population and its resources had been compiled on the basis of sworn inquests, and the same method had occasionally been used for judicial purposes. Now the method was used more regularly and made available partly for administrative inquiries, partly for civil litigation before the king's justices, and partly for the purpose of getting suspected criminals into the clutches of the royal officers.

The king's justices itinerant were often commissioned to inquire into every aspect of local government of interest to the king, into the conduct of the sheriffs, and into grievances of all kinds. The General Eyre, as this kind of inquiry came to be called, was a most formidable affair, and information about every detail was procured from a sworn jury of the hundred, who had to answer, on oath and under severe penalties, all the searching questions put to them by the justices. The *recognitio* or sworn inquest came to be the regular method adopted by the government for getting information about almost any matter. In the judicial sphere proper, the inquest procedure was made available to litigants in disputes concerning the possession of land, then inevitably the principal theme of civil litigation. The facts of the matter were established by the sworn testimony of twelve good and lawful men of the neighbourhood, who were presumed to know the facts. This kind of procedure proved to be far more popular than that of the feudal courts, wherein justice could easily be denied, and wherein the issue was decided by reference to the ordeal of battle, by a duel between the parties or their champions. The time was to come when no man need answer for his land save on a royal writ and by sworn inquest. It is not surprising that the royal justices soon attracted to themselves a mass of land litigation, nor that Henry II and his successors sometimes adopted very high-handed methods of encouraging the process, for *justitia est magnum emolumentum* (justice is great profit). The profits of justice went to swell the royal exchequer.

In criminal jurisdiction, the use of the jury did not as yet extend beyond the presentment by sworn jurors of suspected criminals to the king's sheriffs. It is a doubtful matter how far Henry II was innovating in using juries for this purpose, for the origin of this—the modern grand jury (abolished for nearly all purposes in 1933)—may have been a great deal earlier in fact than the famous Assize of Clarendon of 1166, which certainly set out the principle of the jury of presentment in writing. But suspected criminals were not as yet tried by jury; trial was still by the old methods of ordeal, as in Anglo-Saxon days, although now in the presence of the king's justices. The jury of verdict did not come in until after the withdrawal of the Church's blessing on the ordeal in 1215. For some time after that date nobody quite knew how to try suspected criminals; the ancient idea that the question of guilt was a matter that could only be decided by divine revelation in the ordeal died very hard. It was the king's justices, apparently with little specific guidance from the government, who eventually hit on the notion that if facts in general could be established by the sworn testimony of twelve lawful men of the neighbourhood, then the fact of guilt might as well be established in the same way. From about the middle of the thirteenth century, therefore, the jury of verdict or guilt, the modern petty jury, came into existence, and developed into the most famous of English legal institutions. The king's justices had scored a victory for common sense and for the Crown, whose ultimate triumph in criminal jurisdiction was thereby assured. In the time following, to the king's justices fell the great task of hammering out the common law of England from the welter of diverse local customs and usages. The common law was judge-made, and not made merely by the arbitrary will of the king. By a fortunate turn of events, although the judges were necessarily the king's judges, they were never regarded by their masters as mere civil servants to do the king's bidding. As a distinct legal profession developed in the course of the thirteenth and fourteenth centuries, the king invariably selected his justices from among the profession, and from nowhere else. The duty of the judges thus came to be primarily to the law, not to the will of the king, and they were charged with the duty of maintaining the law, notwithstanding any command of the king to the contrary. In consequence of this remarkable piece of royal wisdom, the judicial bench never became at any time the mere tool of the government, even if later on in the seventeenth century there was to be great danger of such a degeneration.

In these and other ways the monarchy succeeded in developing central government and opening up lines for its further expansion to a degree undreamt of in the past. There were to be many tests and trials ahead, but the ground gained by the end of Henry II's reign was never lost. The first test came very soon after Henry II's death, for during nearly all of his reign Richard I (1189–99) was absent from the realm, either on Crusade, in captivity, or pursuing his ambitions on the Continent. Notwithstanding the unprecedented length of the king's absence, his government was successfully carried on by his officers, not indeed without some trouble with refractory magnates, but at least without any breakdown of the central government. His successor, John

(1199–1216), inherited a strong engine of government which he, being what he was, soon found could be used or abused without consistent regard for principles of justice and good government. His financial needs were great and his political difficulties acute, but his arbitrariness evoked opposition from powerful groups of his baronage. A basic constitutional problem at once arose: How could the king be kept to the letter of the law? The best answer which that generation could make to that question was contained in the most famous of all historical documents—in the Great Charter (*Magna Carta*).

The Great Charter is a disappointing document to those who expect to find in it high-sounding principles and general declarations. The conspiracy of churchmen and barons who by force of arms compelled King John to cause the Great Seal to be affixed to the Charter at Runnymede in June 1215 were not imbued with the Rights of Man or the principles of Liberty, Equality, and Fraternity. They were not concerned with theories of any kind. All they wanted was to put a stop, if they could, to the king's playing ducks and drakes with feudal custom and with certain parts of the other law of the land; they wanted to get the king's seal affixed to a declaration of what the law was, or at any rate of what they thought it ought to be, regarding a number of very specific points, and they wanted to create machinery for compelling the king to keep in future to what he had agreed.

Magna Carta is therefore primarily a feudal document about feudal custom and the rights of tenants-in-chief, but is not exclusively such. John had lost the support of a proportion of the feudal class, and all articulate classes participated in the rebellion in some degree. Every class therefore got something out of the charter. The feudal magnates and their vassals secured definition of some of their rights; the Church got something out of it in its struggle to be free of lay interference and to obey the law of the Church; freemen in general secured definition of their rights in a number of important points; the cities and boroughs got a confirmation of their privileges and the concession of a few points of law of especial interest to them; even the poor unfree serfs got a narrow but useful measure of protection from at least utterly ruinous exactions by the Crown, so long as they were not serfs on the royal demesne. Some legal points of general interest were also set down as part of the agreement—declarations that were destined to be quoted against the Crown during the great conflict of the seventeenth century in ways and for purposes which would have been startling indeed to the barons of Runnymede.

But to make solemn declarations was one thing. It was quite another and a far more difficult thing to compel the king and his officers to keep to what had been agreed. What if the king broke the law, and repudiated or ignored his promises? Who was to remedy such a situation as that, and how was it to be done?

The barons of the Charter were far from being oblivious of these problems. Indeed, the problems were as old as government itself. In theory, the king had always been regarded as below the law, and the right to resist a lawless monarch had always been recognized in ancient Anglo-Saxon and Germanic custom generally. By feudal custom, furthermore, a vassal who was aggrieved by breach of his contract had the right to defy and coerce his lord. But it was in *Magna Carta* that for the first time an attempt was made to record in the written public law the actual setting up of a regular piece of constitutional machinery for coercing the king if he broke the law as contained in the Charter. A committee of twenty-five barons was to be established and authorized to distrain the king (saving the royal person) (i.e. to seize his castles and properties) until he mended his ways if he infringed the terms of the Charter.

Of course, this provision, if it had ever been operated in practice, would have been disastrous. Legalized rebellion is not a satisfactory method of obliging the king's government to respect the law. But in 1215 it was the best method the barons could think of. The development of less violent and more indirect and subtle methods of obliging the king to keep to the law was to be a slow and difficult process spread over the centuries to come; in time the problem came to be closely bound up with a still more difficult aspiration—the desire to compel the government, not only to keep to the law, but also to keep to policies within the law acceptable to the governed. In the end the supremacy of the law had somehow to be reconciled with the supremacy of the people. These problems were eventually to be solved by means and methods beyond the imagination and experience of the men who witnessed the Great Charter. But their efforts were not to be in vain; without their enterprise, the solution to the problems would have been infinitely more difficult, and might never have come at all. The Great Charter has its place in the prehistory of government by consent.

The Struggle between King and Magnates for the Control of Central Government

One of the most remarkable features of the Great Charter episode is the slight degree to which the barons sought to modify the machinery of central government which had been built up by the Crown in the past. It is true perhaps that in one clause an effort was made to restrict the Crown's using one of its means of diverting jurisdiction in land disputes from the feudal courts to the royal courts, and that this provision might have had the effect of impeding the expansion of royal justice in one direction. But the king's lawyers, and the litigants who preferred royal justice, soon found ways and means of evading the restriction, even if at the cost of much technical complication, and there was to be no serious obstacle to the steady development of royal justice.

The character of the Great Charter and the course of history were profoundly modified by the premature death of King John and the accession of a minor in the year after Runnymede. The fact that nearly a quarter of Henry III's long reign (1216–72) was a period of minority, during which the king's government was carried on by someone other than the king himself, was of crucial importance. The government could only be carried on by one representative or another of the baronage, and it was carried on, in the main, with an amazing degree of loyalty. The minority government was inevitably confronted with a quandary. What, in the new circumstances, was to be done with the Great Charter? Some of the clauses intended to prescribe methods of government were not so desirable now that the baronage itself in effect constituted the government. What of the baronial committee of resistance? Were the baronage to coerce themselves or their own nominees? The Charter had been extracted from King John by force. Now it was reissued on behalf of Henry III—with most of the constitutional clauses omitted, including the resistance clause. What was left of it was almost, but by no means entirely, confined to matters of private law, and, as such, it was to be reissued in definitive form in 1225, and reconfirmed many times, and eventually to be enrolled on the statute book. From a document extorted from a most unwilling king, it was transformed into an incontestable part of the law of the land.

It would be reasonable to suppose that the experience gained and the sweets of power enjoyed by the baronage or by part of it during the minority of Henry III encouraged the growth of political consciousness and of the notion that the king's policy might perhaps be controlled in some degree. However that may have been, Henry III's reign saw the rise of political opposition to the Crown, the emergence of genuine constitutional conflict, and, before it was over, some re-orientation occurred of the direction in which the central government was to travel in the future.

The period of Henry III's personal rule (1227–58) marked the zenith of the older style of medieval monarchy. The exercise of the will of the king in government was never again to be quite so free and unfettered, or at any rate so free and unfettered in so wide a sphere of government. Henry III was an unfortunate monarch. He inherited the great machinery of government created by his ancestors; his advisers and capable officers extended its scope and made it work with ruthless energy. But Henry was not personally equal to his heritage; he could not make the machine work for the general advantage. He was deficient in political sense and did not understand the art of governing; possibly he relied too much on the advice of his chosen officials and counsellors, many of whom were able men, but who were not often selected from the baronial class and who failed to gain the confidence of that class and could not maintain a harmonious relationship between the magnates and the king.

We cannot enter here into the details of the Barons' War of 1258–65. The constitutional aims of the barons were only temporarily realized, but were not without profound effects upon the course of development. On the one hand, Henry III had sought, before the civil war began, to escape the baronial influences prevailing during his minority by reviving to the full his predecessors' tradition of ruling partly through the administrative organizations of his Household, especially the Wardrobe, which could readily be used to maintain and give effect to the royal will, in co-operation with the more departmentalized Exchequer and Chancery, which by now had tended to become less purely Household organizations. On the other hand, out of the turmoil of the civil war emerged some expedients in the art and craft of government, which, although minor incidents then, were destined to have a great future before them. The seeds of the future parliament were scattered; some fell by the wayside; some on stony ground; some were devoured by the birds of the air. The tender plant that took root was no perennial, nor even a hardy annual; but for the forcing-house of the king's will, it would never have grown at all. But in time it was to grow beyond the confines of the royal will, and at last to become a mighty tree which overshadowed the Crown itself; its roots were to penetrate into the very sub-soil of the national life; its branches to overhang every part of government. But naturally at that time no one foresaw such things; all that could be seen then was the acorn, and very few, if any, noticed that.

The Household method of sustaining the royal will was carried to very considerable lengths, and there was no one to say that the king could not do as he liked in the matter. It may have been unwise, but it was not in any way illegal. It was not this practice in itself that brought baronial opposition to a head in 1258, although, no doubt, in further divorcing the Crown from the support of any class other than that of its own officials, it contributed to the general result. If Henry III had attained any success in his policies, foreign or otherwise, the story might have been different, but he did not. In the upshot, he was forced to face a temporarily united baronage, and to agree to a radical recasting of the form of government. The Provisions of Oxford of 1258 in effect put the kingship into commission. A baronial committee of fifteen members was to act as a standing organ of government, and to carry on the administration in the king's name. The committee was to meet periodically a selection of the baronage generally to discuss the affairs of the realm. Baronial nominees were immediately installed in the great offices of state.

The scheme duly came into operation; the Fifteen initiated some important reforms in administration, and corrected many evils in local affairs and punished the misdeeds of royal and also baronial officials in the localities. Demands for reforms in private law and administration made by the sub-vassal class, the lesser feudatories, were met (Provisions of Westminster, 1259). But the new Constitution did not last. It was all very well to recall the good old days of the minority, but Henry III was no longer a boy to be kept in leading strings. He may have been foolish, but he was a good wriggler, and he soon wriggled out of the Provisions of Oxford. From the Papacy he secured absolution from his promises, and the arbitration of St. Louis IX of France was in his favour (Mise of Amiens, 1264). In the meantime, the scheme had already collapsed because of dissensions among the barons themselves, and Henry III was adept at playing one faction off against the other. One section, however, headed by Simon de Montfort, Earl of Leicester, who had private quarrels of his own with the king, and who alone among the baronage possibly entertained some political ideas extending beyond those common to his class, would not—probably dared not—acquiesce. De Montfort resorted to arms, and won a brief triumph, defeating and capturing the king and Prince Edward at Lewes, May 1264. Once more the king was put in leading strings, and a small committee of de Montfort's party exercised the government in the king's name. But by August 1265 it was all over; Edward had escaped and, rallying the royal forces, he defeated and slew de Montfort at Evesham. The Crown emerged from the long struggle unscathed, and its prerogatives in government unimpaired. Edward I (1272–1307) was to prove himself one of the greatest and possibly the most powerful of our medieval kings.

But, nevertheless, the scheme of government was never to be quite the same as it had been in the past. For one thing, Simon de Montfort, in bidding for wider political support for his régime, had in 1265 thought it worth while to cause to be summoned in the king's name two knights from each shire and burgesses from various boroughs to meet a number of his magnate supporters. The meeting, in accordance with the usual terminology of the time, was called a parliament, but it was more of a Party convention than anything else, and it can be taken for granted that only people disposed to support de Montfort attended. It was the first time that knights of the shires and burgesses simultaneously attended a meeting of this sort. The meeting was not, however, by any means the origin of parliament nor of representation of local communities at the centre. But it is difficult not to suppose that this incident made its impression upon Edward I and his advisers, for although the expedient was not unknown to the Crown in the days before the Baronial War, it was resorted to more often in Edward I's reign than it had been in the past, and, as the fourteenth century advanced, the representative parliament rapidly became an established feature of the governmental system.

The origins of parliament and the origins of representation of local communities at the centre were two entirely different things; for the earliest parliaments had no representative element at all, and non-representative parliaments continued to be held from time to time even long after representative parliaments had been quite often summoned. The word 'parliament', which in origin meant merely a parley or conference, entered into official language about the middle of the thirteenth century, and was used to designate formal conferences between the king and his officials and a number of the tenants-in-chief summoned personally for the purpose, which, in the main but not exclusively, was to settle difficult judicial questions which for one reason or another could not find solution in the ordinary courts, but which required the exercise of the discretionary power of the king acting with assent. Inevitably other than purely judicial matters came up for consideration. Any policy for which the king wanted the support or at least the views of the magnates might be discussed. This sort of parliament was little more than the old feudal council, and later on, when it became unusual to speak of a parliament without the Commons, assemblies of this kind were commonly called Great Councils. They continued to be summoned from time to time during the fourteenth and fifteenth centuries. The final effort of this sort came in 1640, when Charles I, in a last bid to avoid the wrath of the Commons, summoned a Great Council of peers (as the old feudal class had by that time become), only to be advised by them that the one course open to him was to summon a representative parliament. That was the end of the old Great Councils (except in the form of the House of Lords in a Parliament including the Commons); it was also the end of the medieval monarchy, even though, of course, no one saw it in that light at the time.

The personal summons to the king's court of the great men of the realm was one thing; the summons of elected representatives of the local communities to the centre was another and very different matter. Representation as a governmental expedient for various purposes was ancient even in de Montfort's day. From the point of view of later developments, the most important examples of representation were those which centred around the county courts. In the very early days, all freemen were supposed to attend and constitute the shire courts, but as time passed it became customary for a proportion only of the freemen to undertake the burdens of regular attendance; there was a tendency for the duty to become appertinent to particular pieces of land. But those who attended the court spoke for the county. It has been said, with some exaggeration, that the county court was a parliament in miniature; but at any rate the germs of representation were certainly there. Moreover, in Henry II's time, at full meetings of the shire court held before the king's justices itinerant, each vill in the shire was represented by the reeve and four lawful (i.e. legally respectable) men, and each borough by twelve lawful burgesses. The sworn juries of Henry II's time onwards involved a vague form of representation; in the thirteenth century, to put oneself upon the verdict of the countryside meant to submit to the verdict of a jury. In these and other ways representation must have been a familiar notion in the multifarious affairs of the shire for a very long time before Henry III's reign.

But these representative devices were purely local; to bring local representatives before the king at the centre was a step that had to be taken before anything like a representative parliament could come into existence. This step had already been taken as early as the reign of Richard I, if not earlier, as a mere matter of legal routine. It became the practice, in the event of an appeal of false judgement from a county court, to require the sheriff's record of the judgement to be brought into the king's court by four lawful knights of the shire in person. This in itself was a comparatively trivial matter, but none the less the gulf between the local communities and the king's court had been bridged. By the end of the twelfth century it became quite customary, when the king's court required from a county information which it could not otherwise obtain, for the county court to send it up by the persons of knights of the shire, who spoke for the county, and whose county was penalized if they did amiss. These knights, on whom burdens and responsibilities of this sort were imposed, were the forerunners of the later elected members of parliament.

The device of making spokesmen from the shires come to the centre for governmental purposes was thus no new idea to the Crown or counties in the thirteenth century. As early as 1213 King John (not to be accused of any liberal or democratic notions), being in grave political difficulties at the time, thought it worth while to summon, through the sheriffs, knights from all the shires at once 'to speak with us regarding the affairs of our realm'. We do not know for certain whether this assembly ever actually met, but the stage of a simultaneous summons had been reached. This precedent does not seem to have been followed again until 1254, at a time when Henry III was pursuing his ambitions in Gascony, and the regency at home was obliged to seek wider financial support than usual. It was disappointed in its aims, but it did summon knights from all the shires. The circumstances of the Barons'

War encouraged the notion that one side or the other might secure wider political support by getting representative knights of the shire together to meet the leaders. In 1261 the faction of Leicester and Gloucester in the king's name summoned three knights from each shire to meet them at St. Albans—a summons promptly countermanded by Henry III, who ordered them to meet him at Windsor instead. In 1264, when the king was in his power, de Montfort summoned four knights from each shire to treat of a peace settlement. Burgesses of the boroughs had been summoned on various occasions from John's reign, but it was not until de Montfort's parliament of 1265, already mentioned above, that knights of the shire and burgesses of the boroughs received a summons at the same time.

The utility of this kind of arrangement seems not to have been lost on Edward I and his advisers, for as early as January 1273, whilst the newly-succeeded king was still absent on Crusade, the government brought to the centre four knights from each shire and four persons from the cities, mainly to swear fealty to the king. Moreover, after the king's return, in 1275, both knights and burgesses were summoned to a parliament, and some important legislative and fiscal business was done. But it was twenty years before an assembly of this magnitude was summoned again, and then representatives of the inferior clergy were also included. The precedent of this so-called 'Model Parliament' of 1295 was followed only four more times during the reign of Edward I, whereas non-representative parliaments or parliaments including only some of the elements present in 1295 were summoned on a number of occasions.

It is not easy to determine the motives of the Crown in issuing these occasional summonses of representatives. We may be sure that the general aim was to strengthen the power of the Crown and to improve the efficiency of the government. The particular motives naturally varied according to the needs and circumstances of the moment, and motives were inevitably mixed. It was always valuable to the king's government to get first-hand information as to the conduct of the sheriffs and other royal officers in the localities, and information generally about local government; it was useful to instil into the local representatives a proper sense of respect for the government, and to send them home to spread their impressions of what they had seen and heard at the court of the lord king; on occasions it was worth while to seek the political support of the local communities, especially when there was trouble between the king and any considerable portion of the magnates; sometimes—increasingly often—it was desirable to talk about financial aids and to get the Commons to commit themselves in advance to paying up; it was always an excellent thing to receive petitions and complaints and to provide remedies unobtainable in the ordinary course of the common law; very occasionally it was worth while to get the formal assent of some of them to a piece of legislation, instead of relying solely upon the assent of the greater men. All these and no doubt other motives played their part, but everything depended on the will and initiative of the Crown. Nevertheless, it is quite clear that, from before the end of the thirteenth century, the Crown attached great importance to ensuring that the representatives of the local communities should, when summoned, come fully primed to speak and act on behalf of their communities. The writs of summons were very carefully worded in legally significant language. From 1294 onwards the writs required that the representatives should have 'full and sufficient power to do and consent to those things which then and there by the common counsel of our realm shall happen to be ordained . . . so that for want of such power . . . the affairs may in no wise remain unfinished . . .'. The representatives were to be the attorneys of their communities, with power to bind all those whom they represented in parliament. The formula of the writs remained unchanged in this respect until 1872.

The extraordinary phenomenon in the history of the English parliament (unparalleled in the history of the very similar institutions which came into being in several countries of Western Europe at much the same time) was its development into a representative assembly in a political sense, during the course of the fourteenth, fifteenth, and sixteenth centuries. Parliament began as one aspect of the king's own court; it continued to be that, and in certain respects still is that, but it came to be a great deal more, evolving a political consciousness and an authority derived not from the king's majesty, but from the nation. Born by the irresistible will of the king, it came in time to express the irresistible will of the people.

Into the details of the institutional development of parliament we cannot enter here. We cannot recount how it was that the inferior clergy dropped out and preferred to vote taxes in their own Convocation, leaving the knights and burgesses to coalesce into one lay House of Commons, whilst the great men were transformed into hereditary peers and, with the bishops and other prelates, into members of the House of Lords; how the remarkable and perhaps decisive alliance between the Commons in parliament and the common lawyers occurred, a contingency of the utmost importance for the future stability and development of parliament as an institution; how a Speaker for the Commons, a royal officer to act as an intermediary between them and the king and the lords, appeared; how parliamentary privileges, in time to be of great value as protection against the Crown, developed. Without these and various other developments, almost entirely fortuitous, the modern parliament as we know it could never have come into existence.

But none of these things in themselves would have set the Commons upon the long path to supremacy in the State. That remarkable and unique journey, of some three and a half centuries' duration, did not occur in consequence of any particular ambitions on the part of the Commons, at least not before the seventeenth century. Probably it would not have come about at all but for the crucial fact that in the fourteenth and fifteenth centuries the Commons in parliament proved to be useful pawns to one side or the other in the unending struggle for power between the Crown and the baronial opposition. It was in the course of that long-drawn-out contest that the Commons acquired a political importance and an indispensability for certain purposes, which they could never have attained merely by virtue of the royal writ to the sheriffs ordering them to be elected.

Just as during the period of Henry III's personal rule, so in the first half of the fourteenth century and later, the Crown relied partly upon departments of the Household to supplement the great officers and departments of state. The Wardrobe of the Household attained an even greater place in government under Edward I than under Henry III, with the result that when the strong hand of that masterful king was removed, and he was succeeded by the ineffective Edward II, the fresh phase of baronial opposition took more account of the governmental importance of Household officials. It is doubtful whether the reformers possessed any particular constitutional ideas, but once again, in 1310, the king was forced to agree to the establishment of a baronial committee (the Lords Ordainers), this time to 'ordain and establish the state of our realm'. The Lords Ordainers remained in being for some time; they were a purely aristocratic committee of prelates, earls, and barons, and they promulgated a large number of ordinances, and provided for the appointment of all the great officers, the most important Household officials, by the king by the counsel and assent of the baronage, and *in parliament*. The opposition achieved something in reducing the Wardrobe to little more than a domestic office for the time being, and in making the Keeper of the Privy Seal—the instrument whereby the king issued instructions for the Great Seal in the custody of the Chancellor—less of a domestic and more of a governmental officer.

No phase of baronial opposition lasted very long. Edward II was able to turn the tables on the Ordainers, and he and his advisers succeeded in getting the Ordinances abrogated in a representative parliament, and, moreover, to place on record as a statute the view that, whilst the royal prerogative itself ought to be immune from violence, any necessary reforms of it or in public law ought to be settled in parliaments, by the king and the assent of the prelates, earls, barons, and the Commons (Statute of York, 1322). Opinions may differ as to the precise interpretation to be put on this famous Act, but it is difficult to deny that as a result of it the political importance of the Commons in parliament was promoted.

But violence was not yet spent. Five years later Edward II's enemies succeeded in deposing him altogether—the first deposition since long before the Norman Conquest. It was a *coup d'état* by a faction, but the faithful Commons in parliament were ready to whitewash the transaction, although it was in no sense a parliamentary deposition. When at length Edward III was strong enough to rid himself of his encumbrances, and to exercise the unimpaired powers of the Crown, a further attempt was made to keep control in court hands. Again the fruitful Household brought forth a department, the Chamber, which was used to keep the administration under the royal thumb, much as the Wardrobe had been used in the past. By 1338 an elaborate scheme had been worked out for the centralization of administrative power partly in the Chamber and elsewhere in the Household (Ordinances of Walton).

But the scheme proved to be unworkable in the conditions arising from the war in France; it was too late for the old curialist or household-official type of government to be altogether sufficient in time of continental warfare on a large scale. The administration could not raise enough money or provide adequate support to enable the Crown to carry on its policy of aggrandizement in France. Edward III was obliged to modify his arrangements; to restore a higher degree of authority to the great officers of State, and to accept conditions for the grant in parliament of financial aid. The year 1340 saw a statute enacted in parliament which among other things declared that no charge or aid should be made except by the common assent of the prelates, magnates, and Commons in parliament.

Of course, the Commons themselves took little initiative in these weighty and dangerous transactions. As yet they displayed few political ambitions; it was scarcely possible for them to do so. Parliaments were very short in duration and very infrequent. Back at home the members were inevitably much under the influence of the greater men; the game of politics was apt to be highly dangerous without the support of the powerful. The Commons were not born to greatness; rather they had it thrust upon them. But there is no doubt that the political education of the Commons in parliament proceeded apace in the middle and later fourteenth century. At the least estimate, by then the magnate opposition to the Crown had come fully to realize that the most effective way of bringing the Crown to heel was to act through parliament, and partly through the Commons.

In 1376, for the first time, the Commons (in the Good Parliament) seem to have taken, perhaps partly, though by no means entirely, under aristocratic stimulus, an active part in attacking the government, at that time virtually led by Edward III's eldest surviving son, John of Gaunt (not so much 'time honour'd' as time-serving Lancaster), on behalf of the king, who by then was past the tasks of government. We even begin to hear of impeachment—a procedure of accusation by the Commons and the presentment by them of the alleged offender for trial and sentence by the Lords—an admirable method of using the Commons as cat's paws. But the administration went on much as before.

The struggle between Crown and magnates reached its climax in the reign of Richard II, ending with the capture of the throne itself by the Lancastrian party. Before the end came, the by now almost traditional moves had been played. In 1386 Richard II was forced to agree (in parliament) to being controlled by an aristocratic committee, which, no doubt because it was frightened by the verve and unconcealed hostility of the king, demanded blood. They 'appealed' five of the king's supporters of 'treason' (hence their name of 'Lords Appellant') and Richard felt obliged to summon a parliament in which the accusation was heard. The Merciless Parliament of 1388 duly provided the desiderated judicial murders, and was also remarkable for witnessing the expression by the opposition of notions that in some measure seem to foreshadow, in a vague and inconsistent manner, the later ideas of the supremacy of parliament, but in a judicial as distinct from a legislative sense.

But aristocratic oppositions could never hold together for very long, and in time Richard II had his opportunity for revenge, and took it to the full. Once more, with the co-operation of the dutiful parliament, heads rolled, and the king was to have a period in which to exercise his unfettered prerogatives. But he failed to employ the time to strengthen his position in any positive way, and the end was to come with startling rapidity. A revived faction was headed by Henry Bolingbroke, son of John of Gaunt, who had been banished by Richard II, and deprived of his rights as heir to the Duchy of Lancaster, and who returned ostensibly to claim his inheritance. Whether the result was intended or not, Richard's régime collapsed like a house of cards. Henry bid higher; he claimed the Crown itself. It was a successful *coup d'état* by a faction, but every effort was made to give it the appearance of legality. Richard was forced to abdicate, and a formal deposition was declared by an impressive but vague assembly of 'lords and other people'. There was no deposition in or by parliament; that would have been too much; a parliament was the king's court and existed only by virtue of royal authority, and as yet it was inconceivable that it should get rid of the author of its being, the king.

But with the greatest haste a parliament—consisting of the same people who had been summoned or elected by virtue of Richard II's writs—was assembled in the name of the new king, Henry IV, and this whitewashed the whole transaction. A very careful and elaborate Lancastrian version of the affair was promptly enrolled on its records; the ever-accommodating Commons expressed their wish that Henry IV should have all the 'liberty royal' that his predecessors the kings of England had enjoyed—a wish which Henry immediately granted. Before long, parliaments enacted statutory recognition of the claim of Henry IV's heirs to succeed to the throne.

The magnates had carried opposition to the Crown to its ultimate conclusion; but they had failed to modify the monarchical principle, even if they had tried to do so, which is doubtful; all they had done was to change the dynasty, and put on the throne a line which might be more amenable to their influence. The Commons in parliament had manfully trimmed their sails to the prevailing winds; it was safer that way.

The struggle between king and lords for effective power was continued into the fifteenth century. The contest was now conditioned at first by the fact that Henry IV could not rid himself of the men who had connived at his bid for the throne, and later by the occurrence once again of a long minority, with a consequent struggle between noble factions, ending in a partial collapse of effective government and the setting aside of the Lancastrian dynasty in favour of another line of descendants from Edward III, the Yorkists. Each party in the ascendant found it worth while, indeed indispensable, to make use of the Commons in parliament to give the appearance of legality and respectability to their transactions.

But the true struggle for power centred in the king's council. Whoever could control the council controlled the government, and incidentally decided whether a parliament should or should not be summoned. Henry IV found it very difficult to escape the preponderance of nobles who had supported him, and who naturally expected to share in the power and spoils of the king's government. Even the Commons, anxious to avoid financial demands as far as possible, tried to increase the council's effective power at the expense of the king's will, and on occasion attempted to exercise an abortive power of the purse and to secure redress of their grievances before granting revenue. It was wonderful what the parliamentary antiquarians of the seventeenth century would make of these precedents, but at the time very little came of them.

Friction between Crown and nobles was temporarily eased by Henry V's popular policy of renewed war with France, and but for his premature death in 1422 the course of events at home would doubtless have been very different. The long minority of Henry VI gave a free hand for government by an aristocratic council wielding nearly all the powers of the Crown. For some fifteen years the kingdom had the least effective government it had experienced for three centuries. The lords of the council were too corrupt, too jealous of each other, and probably too amateurish in government to make the administration effective. The decay of central government inevitably resulted in a recrudescence of lawlessness, disorder, maladministration, and corruption on the widest scale. It was not, however, a question of the destruction of the great machinery of government built up in the past; it was rather a question of the failure of the motive power which had always hitherto emanated from the king and his council.

No easy way of reviving the dynamic in government was found. There was some degree of improvement, perhaps, when Henry VI became old enough to assert himself, but Henry VI was no Edward I, and in the long run could not maintain himself against the forces of faction, nor against open competition for the throne itself. His fate at the hands of the Yorkist party was very similar to that of Richard II at the hands of Bolingbroke's faction. There are signs in Edward IV's régime (1461–83) that he understood the necessity for a strong king's council, strong enough to carry out the king's will without fear or favour; it is possible that he learnt from the proposals for administrative reform propounded by the most distinguished adherent of the Lancastrian party.[1] Much was done in his reign to strengthen the financial position and the administrative effectiveness of the Crown. But his reign had to pass, his lawful heirs had to be set aside by his notorious brother Richard III, with the connivance of the Commons in parliament, and yet a new dynasty be firmly settled on the throne by Henry Tudor, also with the assistance of the Commons, before the way was clear for the rehabilitation of good governance by the instillation of renewed energy into the administration, and for the attainment of the zenith of medieval ideals of monarchical government. Under the first Tudor, the medieval constitution reached its climax.

In spite of the worst that violence, faction, and corruption could do and had done during the mid-fifteenth century, the foundations of central government had not in any way been destroyed. The Tudors inherited intact the institutions, the departments, the courts, the common law, and the principle of the supremacy of the law, which had been slowly but solidly built up during the thousand years that had passed since the English had first begun to make their settlement in the island.

But the essential character of the Constitution had changed a good deal during the past two hundred years. The monarchy was

[1] Sir John Fortescue, *The Governance of England*.

no longer conceived of as merely limited by the law. It was not for nothing that on and off for some two centuries the docile Commons had been compelled to journey from their homes to meet the king in his council in his parliaments; it was not for nothing that the great ones of the realm had looked to the Commons in parliament for connivance in high and dangerous policies. Expedients repeated become habits, and habits become customs, and custom can change the law. Parliament had come to occupy a place in the scheme of things which would have been unthinkable a few generations earlier. It had become possible for a professional lawyer and an ex-chief justice of the King's Bench to write with pride and without fear of contradiction: 'Nor does the king [of England], by himself or by his ministers, impose tallages, subsidies, or any other burdens whatever on his subjects, nor change their laws, nor make new ones, without the concession or assent of his whole realm expressed in parliament.'[1]

The king now modified the law of the land and raised taxation, not merely by the assent of the 'wise men' or the 'great men', but of the 'three estates of the realm'—by the 'advice and assent of the lords spiritual and temporal and of the commons, and by the authority of parliament'.

The monarchy had always been regarded as limited by the law. Now it had come to be limited also by the need for the assent of Lords and Commons in parliament for taxation and legislation. Of course, as yet there was not very much taxation (the hereditary revenues of the Crown were still considerable), and not very much important legislation, and therefore parliaments were still few and short, and the Commons, anyway, could usually be relied upon to do as they were told by their betters. Government was still the king's business, and it was not for the Commons to meddle with matters of State and high policy. But within certain limits and for certain purposes the monarchy had become a parliamentary monarchy. Before long the King in Parliament was to encompass the greatest of reforms by abolishing the medieval church. It was to remain for a parliament to abolish the medieval monarchy.

[1] Sir John Fortescue, *De Laudibus Legum Angliae*.

3

Developments in the Sixteenth and Seventeenth Centuries

THE TUDOR RÉGIME IS OFTEN DESCRIBED as the period of the New Monarchy, or as the Tudor Despotism, and regarded as the epoch which saw the foundation of the modern national State. There is a certain amount of justification for these ideas, but not enough to enable us to accept them without a good deal of reservation. The monarchy of the Tudors was not so much new, as rejuvenated; it succeeded in immensely strengthening its executive power, partly by further developing in its service yet another offspring of the Household, the king's secretary, very close to the sovereign and a very pliable instrument of the royal will, destined to a great and remarkable future as the Secretary of State; partly by forming new and effective organs of central government; partly by securing a better hold over local government by relying on the Lords Lieutenant and the Justices of the Peace in the counties; above all by acting in affairs of fundamental importance with the co-operation of Parliaments.

The régime was despotic only in the sense that the two greatest rulers of the House, Henry VIII and Elizabeth, were very autocratic in temper and high-handed in methods, and were not shy, on occasions, of straining and even perverting the law in order to get their own way. But none of them imagined that they were really above the law or that their will alone was the law, and none of them at any time possessed control of sufficient armed forces to impose their will on any large proportion of their subjects. That they were despotic to a degree towards minorities within the state goes without saying; the majority, and perhaps many of the minorities as well, hardly expected them to be otherwise. The Tudor age was not one of political or religious toleration; the despotism of the time was that of public opinion in general rather than of the dynasty.

It is true that the State which the Tudors formed was modern in the sense that it broke the independent power of the Church, and that the sovereigns from Henry VIII onwards found themselves the heads of both Church and State, a position held by none of their predecessors; it was modernized also in the sense of the sixteenth century inasmuch as the power of the executive was expanded to a degree beyond anything imagined in the past. In these respects the Tudor régime in England was in harmony with developments taking place generally in Western Europe at the time. Theories and practices springing from those great changes of mind and attitude conveniently labelled the Renaissance, the Reformation, and the Reception were inevitably, in part at least, very encouraging to the growth of absolutism in government. It was the era during which the modern type of sovereign national states was everywhere emerging; some, where the Protestant views prevailed, becoming supreme over all cases, lay and ecclesiastical, acknowledging no external authority; nearly all developing powerful executives freeing themselves from the trammels of rival authorities within the State. The wide Reception of the principles of Roman Law at this time particularly furthered the doctrines and practices of absolutism in government, and encouraged the idea that the will of the sovereign was law, to the detriment of the old Germanic notion of the supremacy of an impersonal customary law.

All these and other influences had their effects upon Tudor England, but not the effect of breaking down the essential principles of the medieval Constitution, nor even its structure. England became a sovereign national state, with the State supreme over the Church, acknowledging no external authority. Roman law principles had their influence, especially in some of the new courts established by the Crown as part of its plans for an expanded executive, and it may well be that the supremacy of the common law itself was somewhat imperilled. But in point of fact, that supremacy survived unimpaired. The common law of England was not easily to be set aside by 'new-fangled' notions, least of all by alien ideas. It was a very tough kind of law, highly complicated, very unacademic, and closely related to experience and actual needs. The legal profession was by now very well organized and highly trained in its technical craft in its own independent educational establishments, the Inns of Court; from it the king's justices were invariably selected. It was a powerful, proud, and wealthy profession, not at all open to foreign influences and ideas. Moreover, from a very early date, an alliance had imperceptibly grown up between the common lawyers and the Commons in parliament. This remarkable alliance, one of the most fundamental facts in English history, was to prove a decisive factor in the constitutional conflicts of the seventeenth century, and in the long run to give to the English Constitution its most important permanent characteristic—the supremacy of the common law subject only to the overriding legislative power of parliament.

But in the sixteenth century no fundamental constitutional questions were ever raised. The predominant tone was that of harmony between the three great powers within the State—the king's government, the parliament, and the common law. There was as yet little or no rivalry among these three, no conflict for supremacy. The Tudor régime, therefore, was essentially the culmination of the medieval ideals of monarchical government, in alliance with the assent of parliament for certain purposes, and acknowledging the supremacy of the common law where appropriate. No one was concerned about the location of sovereignty within the State. There were signs, in the course of Elizabeth's reign, of friction between the Crown and part at least of the Commons in parliament mostly but not entirely on religious questions, but the marvellous tact of that extraordinary woman, and in the end the general reluctance to thwart the wishes of the venerable Queen by whose devoted labours the realm had been saved from a host of dire perils, served to postpone the pressing of awkward questions. The tacit assumptions, the fundamental principles, and the unsolved problems inherent in the medieval Constitution were to be brought to the test under the Stuarts, and then subjected to the heat of acute controversy, washed in the bloodshed of a civil war, and to be reconsidered in the light of bitter experience, before the Constitution in anything like its modern shape came into being.

The Zenith of the Medieval Constitution

The weakness of the Crown during the fifteenth century had been the source of great evils, the cause of that 'lack of governance and politic rule' that had resulted in a widespread breakdown of the enforcement of law and order, and in a recrudescence of a bastard sort of feudalism, in sporadic civil war. The great Lancastrian chief justice, Sir John Fortescue, had unerringly perceived the reasons for the Crown's ineffectiveness, and had propounded a scheme for administrative reform.[1] No one could have anticipated that the obscure, untried Earl of Richmond, Henry Tudor,[2] who ousted Richard III and succeeded to the throne in 1485, was destined not only to carry into effect wise measures very similar to those foreshadowed by Fortescue, but also to found the greatest of the English dynasties.

Henry VII realized, as the Yorkists had realized, that the weakness of the Crown in the past was the consequence of its poverty, the inefficiency and corruption of its main administrative organ, the Council, and the overweening egotism of the lawless nobility. During his unspectacular but prudent reign (1485–1509), all these evils were overcome, and he was able to pass on to his son, Henry VIII, who was to prove to be a man of unparalleled vitality, energy, and ambition, not only a full Exchequer and a large revenue, but also a Crown far more powerful than ever before, as well as a title to it which, for the first time for a hundred years, was undisputed.

Henry VII raised revenue by every practicable means, mainly within the law, but partly perhaps by abusing legal process and reviving obsolete laws. Crown lands alienated during the civil wars were resumed by parliamentary authority; obsolete or obsolescent feudal and other laws which would raise money if revived were revived; huge fines and forfeitures were imposed for futile rebellions; treason was made financially profitable to the Crown, nor did the king hesitate to speculate in the profits of the then rapidly expanding commercial adventures overseas. It is said that Henry died a millionaire even by contemporary reckoning.

Moreover, the king's Council was no longer suffered to be dominated by great magnates, who inevitably would be concerned with their own interests as much as or more than with the king's, but was composed mainly of capable, ruthless administrators of whatever origins, who could be trusted to put the king's business before all else, and steadfastly to carry out the king's will. Some of them might incur popular odium, but a new administrative aristocracy came into being, who, under the sovereign, were to be the

[1] See above, p. 85.

[2] He was the grandson of the *mésalliance* between Owen Tudor and Katherine of France, widow of Henry V, and son of Edmund Tudor and Margaret Beaufort, who was descended from Edward III through John of Gaunt.

creators of Tudor England. Special steps were taken to strengthen the machinery of the Council in its judicial functions, to suppress lawlessness by whomsoever committed, and to purge the common law of the corruptions which had perverted it. The so-called but wrongly called 'Star Chamber' Act of 1487 was not the origin of the jurisdiction of the Council exercised in Star Chamber—that was inherent in the discretionary authority of the king and his Council. Nor did the tribunal recognized by that Act have much practical effect. The Council, in or outside Star Chamber, dealt vigorously and efficiently with the problems of disorder which had defeated the Lancastrians and had embarrassed the Yorkists.

The decline of the old type of refractory magnate was brought about partly by the force of circumstances, partly by the action of the Crown in clipping the claws of the great. The fifty or so noble families, among whom the Wars of the Roses had been fought, were much exhausted and impoverished by the last quarter of the fifteenth century. The confiscations, the attainders, and the judicial murders that had followed the triumphs of each party over the other inevitably removed some of the leaders of the great houses, and many of the remainder had been slaughtered in the numerous battles of the wars, with the result that many of the old families, if not entirely extinguished in the male line, were by Henry VII's time represented only by minors. The days of feudal, baronial, or aristocratic opposition to the Crown were over. The violent struggles of some two hundred years between the king and the magnates had ended in the overwhelming victory of the Crown. With the ever-growing effectiveness of royal government, and the success with which the law was enforced upon all offenders, no matter how great and powerful, the Crown received a wider and more enthusiastic support than ever before. The people generally were not unnaturally weary of incessant faction fights, fruitless dynastic quarrels, and the unbridled corruption of unscrupulous self-seekers, and rallied with zeal to acclaim and support the young, brilliant, and masterful new monarch, Henry VIII. In the end they were to get from him a good deal more than they anticipated, but none could deny that they got government of a strength and purpose beyond anything imagined in the past.

The Tudor Privy Council became a most powerful organ of government, entirely subordinate to the king, and a highly efficient and tremendously energetic instrument of the royal will.

The range of its interests and the scope of its business were almost beyond belief. The whole field of public and private life came within its purview; no matter was too great or too small to receive its attention, if it once deemed it to be a matter of 'government'—and the broadest possible interpretation was put upon the word, especially after the religious Reformation, when all sorts of ecclesiastical matters, moral questions, and minute points of public and private conduct were deemed to be in that category. Measures for the defence of the realm, the defeat of the Spanish Armada, the defence of the Scots Borders, the safety of the narrow seas, the regulation of trade, financial provisions, questions of high policy, jostled side by side on the Council's agenda with consideration of the matrimonial difficulties of the most obscure citizens, the correction of 'lewd and naughty words', the punishing of the eating of meat in Lent, the revision of unsatisfactory interpretations of the Scriptures, and countless other topics. Offences against the public peace, treasons, rebellions, and disorders of all kinds, however petty, were its especial concern, and part of its jurisdiction in such matters was carried on with relentless care by its committee sitting in what soon came to be called the court of Star Chamber. 'I will make a Star-Chamber matter of it; if he were twenty Sir John Falstaffs, he shall not abuse Robert Shallow Esq. . . . The Council shall hear of it; it is a riot.'[1] In these most apt words, Shakespeare reveals his consciousness of the inexhaustible zeal of Council and Star Chamber. Was he aware that but for that mighty instrument of government the chances are that the peace and security and environment so needful for the blossoming and free expression of his incomparable genius, might—almost certainly would—have been lacking?

The Tudor Council was arbitrary and meddlesome in the highest degree, ruthless and harsh; it resorted to torture; it devised new punishments which it thought fitted the offence. But it was incorruptible and tireless; dealt out justice according to its lights to all alike, to the great and the small, rich and poor, and did much to help the weak and the needy against the oppressions of the strong and wealthy. It was often cruel and unjust, but it served the Crown and the State with unremitting ardour; it enormously enhanced the social coherence of the community; it extinguished anarchy within the realm, and helped to preserve its independence under attack from without.

[1] *Merry Wives of Windsor*, I. i.

Parliament did not play any prominent part in the régime of Henry VII. The docile, time-serving performances of the Commons in parliaments during most of the fifteenth century can hardly have enhanced its reputation as a political assembly. With the decline of aristocratic opposition to the Crown in the last three decades of the century, parliament receded further into the background, to be brought out only for formal legislative and fiscal purposes. In Henry VI's reign there had been twenty-two parliaments in thirty-nine years; Edward IV summoned only seven parliaments in the twenty-two years of his reign; Henry VII managed with the same number in his twenty-four years. The early years of Henry VIII's reign saw very few parliaments; Wolsey seems to have had little taste for representative parliaments, and during the seven years 1515–22 none was summoned. In all the thirty-eight years of the reign (1509–47) only nine parliaments were assembled. Nevertheless, nothing was lost in the way of such constitutional rights as the parliament had acquired in the past, and, as events turned out, its importance and place in the scheme of things were far greater by the end of Henry VIII's reign than they were at its beginning. New life and tremendous vigour were instilled into parliament by that robust king, for his own ends. King in Parliament learnt to legislate away the power of the Papacy within the realm, and thus in co-operation worked the greatest of revolutions, made the State supreme over the Church, and therefore enormously increased the power of the Crown and the prestige and significance of the parliament. For the first time King in Parliament manifested an omnicompetent power.

In order to appreciate the magnitude of the work of the Reformation Parliament of 1529–36, it is necessary to glance back at the relations of Church and State in the past. In medieval theory, in its maturity, State and Church were regarded as two co-extensive organisms. Everyone, except the Jews, necessarily was a member of both. Church and State were two aspects of the same society, but were far from being identical. Each possessed its own head, its own laws and legislative machinery, its own courts of judicature, and its own proper sphere of action. Neither was supreme over the other, neither independent of the other. In England, the normal relations of the two had been peaceful and co-operative, even though for centuries there had been a sporadic borderline conflict over the precise limits to their respective jurisdictions, and over the degree to which the secular power should interfere in a matter vital to both—the selection of the bishops and other prelates, who inevitably occupied positions of influence and power in the temporal as well as the spiritual sphere. Moreover, the Church in England was naturally only a part of the Church Universal, and acknowledged the supreme authority and the appellate jurisdiction of the Papacy. The professional desire of the clergy to obey the behests of the head of the Church and to follow out the rules of the canon law was natural enough, but on occasions it had brought them, or some of them, into conflict with the Crown, especially with regard to Papal appointments to ecclesiastical offices, and with regard to appeals from the Church courts to the Papal *Curia*. In the fourteenth century King in Parliament had intervened in these matters without being considered heretical or schismatic. The Statutes of Provisors of 1351 and 1390 imposed restrictions upon Papal provisions or appointments to the higher ecclesiastical offices in England, whilst the Statutes of *Praemunire* of 1353 and 1393 forbade appeals to Rome in cases in which the Crown had an interest.

The Church had always played a great part in secular government, and the alliance between king and bishops had nearly always been very close. The spiritual magnates, the archbishops, the bishops, and the greater abbots and priors, as tenants-in-chief, had always formed at least half, often more than half, of the feudal council, and had come to constitute a majority in the Upper House of Parliament. Representatives of the inferior clergy were summoned to the parliaments, but ceased to come from about 1330, and, instead, attended in the two provincial Convocations of Canterbury and York. There they granted their own share of taxation to the Crown, and legislated in spiritual matters, making canons which were enforceable in the Church courts upon clergy and laity alike.

The ecclesiastical courts enjoyed an extensive jurisdiction. They possessed exclusive jurisdiction over the clergy, not merely in ecclesiastical offences, but also in all temporal offences, including felonies, except treason. Furthermore, their jurisdiction over laity and clergy included all testamentary and matrimonial causes, and all moral causes, which then covered such matters as slander and libel. The sanctions imposed in these courts were spiritual, but in some instances they might have temporal consequences as well—degradation from holy orders, penance, or excommunication, as might be appropriate, and the long arm of the secular power was available to bring the recalcitrant offender to heel, if necessary.

Most of this system of ecclesiastical jurisdiction remained in operation long after the Tudor Reformation. In time, the jurisdiction over the laity passed to the ordinary courts, and although the Church of England today still possesses courts, their jurisdiction is confined to minor matters of ecclesiastical interest only. Moreover, long before the Tudor régime was over, the Church of England had acquired a new master—the Crown.

We cannot here consider the underlying causes of the Reformation in England, nor the motives of Henry VIII in destroying the Papal power, nor even the question of the king's divorce, which was the occasion rather than the cause of the break, still less the development of diverse religious opinions in the later Tudor period. We are concerned only with the broad fact that the abolition of the Papal authority in England was legalized by parliamentary enactment. Before the main attack on that authority was launched, Henry VIII set about silencing the inevitable opposition of the clergy by threatening to apply to them a very broad interpretation of the Statute of *Praemunire* of 1393, and to exact very severe penalties for the alleged infringement of it by the bishops and clergy. The threat was devastating, and most of the higher clergy were glad enough to purchase pardon in exchange for a large financial contribution and an acknowledgement that the king was 'the singular protector, only supreme lord, and as far as the law of Christ allows, even supreme head, of the Church and clergy of England' (1531). A number of statutory restrictions on ecclesiastical jurisdiction and privilege had already been made, and now Act after Act was passed demolishing the Papal powers within the realm, and establishing those of the Crown instead. The financial tribute paid hitherto to 'the Bishop of Rome, otherwise called the Pope' was either abolished or diverted to the Crown. The Act in Restraint of Appeals of 1534 denied in its preamble the authority within the realm of any external power, temporal or spiritual, and provided that all spiritual causes were henceforth to be finally adjudged and determined within the realm. By another Act of the same year, the legislative independence of Convocation was terminated. The Act of Supremacy of the same year recognized the authority of the Crown over all persons and causes, and declared the king to be 'the only Supreme Head in earth of the Church of England, called *Anglicana Ecclesia*'. An

Act of 1536 extinguished any remnants of Papal authority in England and imposed severe penalties on anyone bold enough to defend it in future.

The work of the Reformation Parliament, which remained in being for the unprecedentedly long period of nearly seven years, was thus stupendous in its achievements and implications. It had co-operated with the Crown in legislation of the greatest magnitude and importance. The subsequent Acts dissolving the monasteries were trifles compared with what had already been done, but the consequential removal of the mitred abbots and the greater priors ended for ever the ecclesiastical majority in the House of Lords. It is not surprising, but very significant, to find Henry VIII himself declaring to representatives of parliament in 1543 that 'We be informed by our judges that we at no time stand so highly in our estate royal as in the time of parliament, wherein we as head and you as members are conjoined and knit together into one body politic.'

The Commons in parliament had at long last come into high favour with the Crown, which sought to increase their prestige, to extend their privileges, and to share with them the onus (and the odium) of high policies. There was not, of course, as yet any suggestion that government was any other than the king's business; it was not supposed that the Commons had anything much to do but debate, accept, or reject—perhaps occasionally to modify—the government's proposals; it was not for them to initiate important matters nor to debate questions of high policy not put before them by the Crown.

As yet there was no doctrinal reform in religion. All that had happened so far was the substitution of the Crown for the Papacy as the supreme authority over the Church. When, after Henry VIII's demise, the time came for doctrinal reform, it was a matter for the exercise of the royal supremacy, using parliamentary enactment when appropriate. By these means the doctrinal changes under Edward VI (1547-53), Mary (1553-8), and Elizabeth (1558-1603) were accomplished in accordance with the views of these sovereigns, with little regard for the increasingly diverse opinions of many of their subjects. The Elizabethan Church settlement, which, because it was a compromise in doctrinal matters, has remained basic to the Anglican Church ever since, was legalized by the two great Acts of 1559, the Act of Supremacy and the Act of Uniformity. The former Act recognized the Queen as Supreme Governor of the realm as well in all spiritual or ecclesiastical things or causes as temporal; the latter imposed uniformity of religious observance under penalties. The king has remained titular governor of the Church of England, but the modification of the rules of uniformity became a burning question in the politics of the ensuing two and a half centuries.

The Reformation Parliament of 1529–36 was the first parliament to remain in being for a protracted period, and was consequently the first to give the Commons a substantial opportunity to develop a sense of corporate experience and an *esprit de corps*. It was now becoming increasingly common for members to be re-elected, and in this period there are many signs that a seat in the House was becoming an object of ambition, instead of being regarded, as in the earlier days, as a burden to be avoided if possible. Knights of the shire now frequently sought to be elected for a borough. At times there were manifest efforts on the part of the Crown to secure the election of members likely to favour and advance the royal policies. The number of constituencies was considerably increased. Henry VIII incorporated Wales and Chester into the parliamentary system, and a number of new parliamentary boroughs were created, especially under Elizabeth, with the result that the 298 seats which had comprised the first House of Commons of Henry VIII's reign became 467 by the time of James I. The franchise in the counties remained (and continued to remain until 1832) as it had been fixed by a statute of 1430—vested in men possessing freehold of the annual value of forty shillings. In the early fifteenth century this constituted a considerable sum, but the value of money had fallen, so that the effective franchise had widened, and it was not so easy for the Crown to influence county elections. It was less difficult to do so in the boroughs, in which the franchise varied widely according to the terms of the charter of incorporation and to the customs of the boroughs. Elizabeth showed marked zeal in creating new parliamentary boroughs, especially in the south-west, no doubt in the hope of ensuring the return of well-disposed members; later on, Charles II and James II were to go to extremes in fixing borough elections, and were thus able to do a good deal by way of 'packing' the Commons, for the number of borough representatives greatly exceeded that of the counties'. But as yet the Crown felt little need for efforts of this kind, and the Tudor parliaments were not packed to any important extent. The general influence of the Crown over the

Commons and the particular influence of privy councillors in the Commons were still sufficiently great to make such attempts unnecessary. The Commons were nearly always content to follow the lead of the government, although occasionally they could and did resist the wishes of the Crown, and compelled it to think again. In the main, however, the prevailing note was one of harmony, particularly during the highly dangerous even if exhilarating times of Elizabeth. Henry VIII had, of set policy, done much to develop and define the privileges of the House. As yet the Crown had no fears of the parliament, and was disposed to strengthen it and to make it as reputable as possible. The privilege of freedom of arrest during session was very much better defined during this period, and came to be enforceable by the House itself. Even the privilege of freedom of speech was exalted by Henry VIII. It was doubtless very useful to him to be able to instruct his agents at the Papal *Curia* in 1532 to reply to the Pope or the Cardinals if they took exception to the Act in Restraint of Annates that 'debate in our parliament is free, and it is not possible for us to interfere in their discussion about any matter, and forsooth they decide as they think fit according to what they deem to be the profit or otherwise of the State'.

But to Elizabeth, who by force of circumstances was often obliged to pursue policies too subtle and tortuous for the simple Commons to apprehend, freedom of speech in the House seemed to be fraught with dangers and inconveniences. She did not object to reasonably free debate of the matters put before the Commons by the Crown, but she constantly warned them off such matters of very high policy as religion, foreign affairs, and the delicate question of the succession to the throne. She was not prepared to admit that the privilege of freedom of speech meant freedom to discuss *any* topic, but only such topics as she thought suitable. When the fruits of her endeavours on behalf of the realm had been won, the Spanish menace had been disposed of, and the worst dangers from religious dissension and treasonous plots had passed, the Commons began to show less acquiescence in her high-handed dealings with them. They forced her to beat a retreat on the question of the grant of monopolies by the Crown, and showed restiveness in other directions as well. But it was impossible that there should have been a sustained quarrel between them and the greatest of queens. Elizabeth's personal presence and the delivery of one of her gracious speeches, superb in word, thought, and manner, were quite sufficient to still the hot words on the lips of the faithful and fervently loyal Commons, and to bring hot tears into their eyes instead.

The time was not yet ripe for serious conflict between Crown and parliament. But that parliament had attained a great place in the scheme of things is well shown in the words of Sir Thomas Smith, who became one of Elizabeth's Secretaries of State. 'The most high and absolute power of the realme of England', he wrote, 'consisteth in the Parliament. . . . For everie Englishman is entended to bee there present, either in person or by procuration and attornies, of what preheminence, stage, dignitie, or qualitie soever he be, from the Prince (be he King or Queene) to the lowest person of Englande. And the consent of the Parliament is taken to be everie mans consent.'[1]

Part of the secret of the extraordinary success achieved by the Tudors is to be found in the degree to which they were able to make their powerful will felt in local government. The great days of the sheriffs as the local representatives of the Crown were over; the temptations and corruptions to which they had always been exposed, and to which they had largely succumbed during the fifteenth century, undermined their position. Under the Tudors the sheriffs receded into the background, and effective power and trust passed to the new Lords Lieutenant of the counties, and to the local Justices of the Peace. The Lords Lieutenant became the most dignified royal officers in the shires, and took over the military headship of their counties, and various other duties in connexion with the conservation of the peace of the shires. But the main burden of local government now fell upon the Justices of the Peace, a local magistracy of local gentry of good position well versed in local affairs. They were not a Tudor creation, being derived originally from the conservators of the peace who appeared at the end of the twelfth century, and more directly from statutory creations of 1360. But under the Tudors they became the chief pillars of local government and the favourite agents of the central government in the localities. Upon them was imposed a wide and ever-increasing range of both judicial and administrative duties, which gave them positions of great local importance and influence. But they were in no sense civil servants; they were unpaid for their invaluable services, which were voluntarily undertaken. The Justices of the Peace were thoroughly characteristic of

[1] *De Republica Anglorum*, written 1562–6, published 1583.

the masterly Tudor methods of government. The training and experience they gained in the performance of their multifarious duties, together with the political experience that many of them acquired as members of Parliament—for the Commons were usually elected from the very same class which furnished the Justices of the Peace—went far to produce a remarkable social stratum of men of independent means, of much experience of law and administration, of mature political consciousness, and ambitious to play a part in government. They served the Tudors well, for harmony was the general tone in the relations between the king's government and the majority of the people. If once that harmony should come to be broken down, the Crown might find itself faced with disaster, for it would be able to rely upon no local instruments of government other than the Justices of the Peace, who could be compelled to do nothing, but who, with their class generally, might prove themselves to be most formidable political opponents.

Conflicts of Principle

The seventeenth century is the Heroic Age in English Constitutional History. The hitherto prevailing harmony between the three authorities within the Constitution—the Crown, the Parliament, and the Courts of Common Law—broke down during the first three decades of the century, primarily because of fundamentally different interpretations of the Constitution adopted by the Crown on the one side, and the Commons and common lawyers on the other. For the time being the Crown was the stronger, and its supremacy over the other parts of the Constitution was established during the fourth decade. But this supremacy could not in the long run be maintained in the face of extraordinary political circumstances, and gave way to a short-lived restoration of something like the Tudor balance of powers during the first year of the Long Parliament (1641). This balance might perhaps have been sustained indefinitely but for the rise of acute religious differences between the Crown and the militant Puritan party in the Commons. It was essentially the desire to control the religious policy of the Crown that inspired the further and far more extreme constitutional conflicts which resulted in the complete breakdown of co-operation between Crown and Parliament, and the resort of both sides to armed force. This fratricidal struggle was to involve in the end resounding events which no one foresaw at the outbreak of the Civil War—the exercise of executive power by what came to be left of the Parliament, the judicial murder of the king himself, the abolition of the monarchy and of the House of Lords, and the establishment of a military dictatorship which was to seek in vain to convert itself into a civil authority commanding a civil allegiance. The failure of this attempt, and the unsuccessful constitutional experiments of the Interregnum (1649–60), brought the country back to the point in 1641 at which it had departed from its historic path, and the ancient triumvirate of King, Parliament, and Common Law was restored—but without their old harmony. At the Restoration of 1660 no attempt was made to define the proper relations between these three authorities. Even if a serious attempt of the kind had been made, it is inconceivable that any agreement could have been reached among the parties so soon after the Civil War. The old institutions were therefore restored, but no awkward questions were asked as to the relations between them. It soon became manifest, however, that those relations were not going to be the same as in the old days. The Crown now could evade the efforts of Parliament at controlling the policy of the executive only with great political difficulties and financial strain. Charles II did eventually succeed in shaking off the unwelcome efforts of Parliaments, and there is no telling what perversion of the Constitution might have ensued but for his own premature death, and the crass stupidity of his brother James II in pursuing a religious policy so totally unacceptable to all parties of importance that the consequent Revolution of 1688–9 was both bloodless and final. It was bloodless because no one would strike a blow for a lost cause, and it was final because the ensuing settlement made the minimum possible departures from tradition, modified the law in one or two points upon which both the Tories and Whigs were agreed, and left the rest to time and chance. The result was the firm establishment of King, Lords, Commons, and Courts of Common Law, each possessing rights of their own, each dependent upon the others in certain respects, each with an indispensable part to play in the government of the realm.

The Constitutional Law of England has, of course, been modified in many particulars since that date, but it has never been altered in a fundamental respect from that day to this. The law remains basically the same now as then. What has changed out of all comparison are the relations between the parts of the

Constitution, and these relations have been in the main changed, not by legal reform, but by the development of conventions unforeseen then, but which have been evolved out of experience and the practical needs of changing political circumstances.

The period from the accession of James I in 1603 to the year 1629 witnessed a struggle—in the main a successful struggle—on the part of the Crown to assert its dominance over both the Parliament and the Common Law. It was to some extent a struggle of personalities. The characters of James I, and from 1625 of Charles I, of Queen Henrietta Maria, of the royalist lawyer Francis Bacon, of the common lawyer Edward Coke, of Pym and Eliot in the Commons, of Archbishop Laud, and of Thomas Wentworth, Earl of Strafford, and of many others, all contributed elements to a struggle which would have been very different if those characters had been different. But it was also a struggle of incompatible principles and points of view. Both sides in the contest appealed to law and history, but it was the royalist side which then represented the modernist, progressive opinion, whilst the parliamentary opposition and the common lawyers looked to the 'good old days' of the medieval constitution for precedents to support the supremacy of the Common Law and the partnership of Parliament in the Constitution against the magnification of the royal prerogative and the dominance of the executive power. The Crown based its case largely upon a comparatively new-fangled theory of the divine hereditary right of the monarch to rule, which, in so far as it was carried to its logical extreme, was incompatible with medieval notions of limited monarchy, the rights of Parliament, and the ultimate supremacy of the Common Law. It based its case also upon the general tendency everywhere in Europe to free the executive power in the State from hampering restrictions and to establish monarchies absolute in theory and in practice. The common lawyers and parliamentarians who opposed this powerful impulse to aggrandize and sanctify the executive power could find little comfort and support except by looking back to the past, and seeking there material and precedents which seemed to confound the arguments of the royalists. That many historical events were falsified in this process goes without saying; most of the grist brought to the mill by the opposition out of *Magna Carta* and the parliamentary records of the fourteenth and fifteenth centuries does not bear serious examination. But the attitude of these opponents of the Crown was to have a permanent influence upon the fundamental character of English political life, and it was to be one of the many paradoxes in English history that the resisters to Stuart monarchy were cast in a highly conservative mould, and looked to the historic past for weapons with which to combat the tendencies of their time. But many medieval precedents were ambiguous, and the Crown was often able to confound its critics by appeal to the letter of the law, and by securing an interpretation of the law favourable to itself.

James I was not only a Scot, brought up in a constitutional environment entirely alien to that into which he was transferred in his larger kingdom, but, what was worse, he was also a scholar of more learning than discretion. Not content with merely adopting a theory of the divine right of hereditary kingship, he felt impelled to compile a voluminous tome setting out his views and arguments on the theme at great length, as well as to improve, as he thought, every occasion by expounding his doctrines. That this unfortunate habit of philosophizing, in season and out of it, helped to focus and harden opinion against him cannot be doubted, but at least he was less intransigent than his son Charles I was to prove, and during his reign (1603–25) the extremities of conflict were avoided. Nevertheless, his views as to the place of the Crown in the Constitution inevitably brought him into sharp contest with the other co-existent authorities, the Common Law and the Parliament, and set up the alignments of parties, powers, and forces that were to make the Civil War of 1642–9 possible.

The independence of the Common Law found its champion in the person of the redoubtable Sir Edward Coke, who had been a highly royalist Attorney-General under Elizabeth, but who, as chief justice, first of the Common Pleas and later of the King's Bench, became the very embodiment of the spirit of the Common Law, and was destined to immortal fame as an antagonist of the Crown, both on the Bench and in the Commons, and also as a medium by which the continuity of the Common Law was preserved, and the medieval law merged into the modern.

In several cases of constitutional importance in which James I sought from the judges a decision or opinion favourable to the Crown, Coke stood out against him. The details need not detain us here, but the essential principle at stake was whether the judges were merely civil servants or whether their primary duty was to interpret the law. That they were in fact the king's servants was indubitable, and there were no means of preventing the king from dismissing Coke from the chief justiceship of the King's Bench in 1616, but in taking such a step James I set his dynasty on a course that was in the end to prove disastrous. Coke's judicial career was terminated, but he was still to add his powerful support to the opposition in the Commons, and his spirit was to live on in his legal writings long after the Stuarts had ceased to reign.

James I's views and the tactlessness with which he expressed them brought him into conflict with each of his four parliaments. Perhaps he was technically right in asserting that the privileges of the Commons existed, not as of right, but by the king's grace, but the point was somewhat academic, and it was politically unwise to press it, and this and other differences of opinion gave birth in 1604 to the first of the great documents of the period which set out the Commons' view of their position. *The Form of Apology* purported to state and to correct what they considered to be the king's misapprehensions of several constitutional points of importance, including the question of the nature of parliamentary privilege.

It was primarily through finance that the Commons could hope to exert pressure upon the Crown, for its pecuniary necessities were great and increasing. The days when the Crown could carry on its government in normal circumstances largely out of its hereditary revenues were gone. For a long time the consequences of a general fall in the value of money had been felt, even if not understood. Elizabeth's finances in her later years had been still further upset by the high cost of dealing with an Irish rebellion, and she left a considerable debt behind her, as well as a heavy annual deficit. It is not surprising therefore that James I sought ways and means of increasing his revenue; it was rather his method of doing so that aroused opposition and misgivings.

The legal right of the Crown to impose additional customs duties for the purpose of regulating trade was not doubted, but it had not been envisaged that this power might be turned to the purpose of raising substantial revenue outside parliamentary consent. The legality of the Crown's action in raising new duties was brought to the test in Bates's case in 1605, and the decision of the judges was in the Crown's favour. The ruling was probably sound enough according to the letter of the law, but several of the judges included in their judgements unfortunate passages that seemed to echo the king's own political sentiments, and James himself followed up with some very high-sounding observations on the matter. His subsequent command to the Commons 'not to dispute of the King's power and prerogative in imposing upon merchandises exported or imported' provoked a vigorous claim by them that it is 'an ancient, general, and undoubted right of Parliament to debate freely all matters which do properly concern the subject and his right or state; which freedom of debate being once foreclosed, the essence of the liberty of Parliament is withal dissolved'.

In short, the Commons were no longer disposed to accept the Tudor interpretation of the parliamentary privilege of freedom of speech, and a great debate on impositions took place notwithstanding the king's command to the contrary. Eleven years later, the insistence of the Commons on debating James's unpopular foreign policy brought the dispute to its climax. The king's command to refrain evoked the great Protestation of 18 December 1621:

> That the liberties, franchises, privileges, and jurisdictions of Parliament are the ancient and undoubted birthright and inheritance of the subjects of England; and that the arduous and urgent affairs concerning the King, State, and defence of the realm, and of the Church of England, and the maintenance and making of laws, and redress of mischiefs and grievances which daily happen within this realm, are proper subjects and matter of counsel and debate in Parliament; and that in the handling and proceeding of those businesses every member of the House of Parliament hath, and of right ought to have, freedom of speech to propound, treat, reason, and bring to conclusion the same . . .

James could, and did, dissolve the Parliament, send for the Journals, and with his own hand tear out these resounding words, but he could not set back the clock. He could not revive Elizabethanism. He could not restore harmony where now discord prevailed. Already the Commons had resorted to the old procedure of impeachment and struck at two of the king's ablest officials, Francis Bacon, the Lord Chancellor, and Lionel Cranfield, the king's financial adviser. In both cases the main charges related to corruption, but an attack by the Commons upon the king's ministers was ominous. The stage was being set for more tragic scenes.

No issues were solved under James I, but the parties were taking up their positions for the greater conflict to come. On the one side stood the king with his large and ill-defined prerogative powers, his potent executive instruments in the Privy Council and its judicial offshoots, Star Chamber, Court of High Commission, and others, and with his ultimate control over the Bench, supported by the bishops and the episcopalian party in the Church of England and royalists generally; on the other side stood those common lawyers who did not favour royalism, and the anti-royalist Puritan element inside and outside the Parliament, with no weapons but the negative one of refusing financial aid, and the destructive one of impeachment, both of which could be wielded only in Parliament.

The accession of Charles I (1625–49), a man who was incapable of learning wisdom from experience, did nothing to smooth the troubled political waters. The relations between the Crown and the Commons rapidly deteriorated, and sharper notes were sounded. The conflict between them now turned mainly on the crucial question of finance. The intention of the Commons to apply severe pressure to the Crown was clearly shown by the unprecedented action of Charles's first Parliament in proposing to grant tunnage and poundage (the usual customs duties on imports) for one year only, instead of for life as was customary. The fact that a life grant had come to be customary enabled the Crown to continue to levy it on the ground of prescriptive right, notwithstanding that even the proposed grant for one year fell through altogether in the end. The second Parliament of the reign (February to June, 1626) refused to authorize any grant without the prior redress of grievances, and began an impeachment of the king's favourite but incompetent minister, the Duke of Buckingham. To save him, Charles dissolved the Parliament, but more revenue he had to have.

The Statute of Benevolences of 1484 forbade the compulsory exaction of monetary gifts from the people, but there was no law to stop the Crown from accepting loans from its subjects, and it had at its disposal all manner of means of persuading people to offer loans. To this desperate expedient of exacting 'forced loans' Charles now turned. All kinds of pressure were put upon individuals to lend money to the Crown; poor men were forced to serve as soldiers, or their homes were disturbed by the billeting of troops upon them; rich men were arrested under warrants of the Privy Council if they declined to contribute, and imprisoned whilst they thought it over. A large sum of money was raised in this way, but the judges gave no countenance to the loan, and Chief Justice Crew, who refused to admit its legality, was dealt with as Coke had been dealt with, and was dismissed. But the law as yet offered no remedy to those imprisoned for refusal to co-operate in the loan. The case of the Five Knights (or Darnel's case) of 1626 did not end in a denial by the judges that the king's special command was sufficient authority in law for imprisonment, nor did it result in bail being allowed to the sufferers.

The abject failure of Charles's and Buckingham's incursions into foreign politics compelled the summons of a third Parliament in March 1628, in order to procure further financial supplies. Its meeting was preceded by the release of seventy-six persons who had been imprisoned for non-compliance with a request for a loan. Of these, twenty-seven were returned as members of the new Parliament; this circumstance and the inconclusive nature of the Five Knights' case made it inevitable that the Commons should proceed at once to attack arbitrary imprisonment and arbitrary taxation. They entered into a conference with the Lords upon 'some ancient fundamental liberties of the kingdom'. An attempt to impose statutory restrictions upon the Crown in these matters was foredoomed to failure, and it was under Coke's lead that the method of proceeding by Petition of Right was adopted. There was no precedent for seeking the remedy of public grievances by using the Petition of Right procedure normal in private affairs, and the king did all he could to avoid giving more than a generally affirmative answer to it. But the Petition had passed both Houses, and public agitation was great. In the end, the Commons had their wish, and the response of the Crown in the form *Soit droit fait come est desiré* combined parts of the customary assenting words to both a petition of right and a private bill. But Charles was justified in believing that this assent said no more than his first affirmation implied, for no assent to a petition of right could alter the law. The law remained the same as it had been before, but it was at any rate something to have got a declaration that no man should be compelled to make any gift, loan, benevolence, or tax without common consent by Act of Parliament; that no freeman should be detained in prison without cause shown; that soldiers should not be billeted upon people without their assent. Still, pious declarations were one thing; the means with which to enforce them in practice were quite another thing, and many troubles were to ensue before the means were found.

Mollified in some degree by this success, the Commons prepared a Bill to grant the Crown substantial financial aid, but none the less proceeded with a remonstrance against Buckingham, and prayed for his dismissal. There was no precedent for attacking a Minister save by way of impeachment, which involved some sort of criminal accusation. No crime could be alleged against Buckingham, and Charles answered the remonstrance with a prorogation. In the interval, Buckingham was assassinated, but on the reassembly, the opposition, so far from being quieted, took a new and more defiant turn. To the financial question was now added a religious question. For a long time, the religious policy of the king, episcopalian and High Church in character—some thought pro-Papal—had been increasingly unacceptable to the growing Puritanism of a large proportion of the Commons and of the country. On their reassembly on 20 January 1629, the Commons proceeded to pass resolutions antagonistic to the Crown's religious policy, and to debate questions arising out of the Crown's continuing to levy tunnage and poundage by prescriptive right alone. The king ordered an immediate adjournment, but the Speaker was forcibly held down in the chair, and the Commons passed their resounding resolutions, whilst the king sent for his guard to break into the House.

The Commons had openly defied the king's lawful authority, and the dissolution which followed, on 10 March 1629, dissolved not only the Parliament, but also an epoch. The ancient harmonious balance between the three great powers in the State was at an end. Judges had been dismissed because they would not serve the king alone; the Commons would not grant the financial support necessary to the carrying on of the king's government, and had sought to impose their policy upon the Crown; the king sent the Parliament packing, and was to summon no more—for eleven years.

The only serious practical difficulty in doing without Parliaments was the financial problem. There was no question but that the Crown was vested with all the powers necessary for carrying on the executive government; indeed, no executive power other than the Crown's existed. The assent of both Houses of Parliament was, it is true, necessary for making statutes, but it was easy enough to do without new statutes. Even the financial difficulty could be, and was, largely overcome. Tunnage and poundage continued to be levied by prerogative power, and persons who resisted were dealt with by Council or Star Chamber; there was plenty of room in the prisons. Obsolescent laws were revived and enforced when financial profit would result; monopolies were granted, and ship-money—in the past a lawful method of raising contributions to the Navy from sea-port towns—was exacted from inland towns on the dubious plea of war emergency, and seven of the twelve judges in John Hampden's case (1637) pronounced the exaction to be lawful. As a result of all these measures, the royal finances were much augmented, and by 1638 came to be in a more flourishing condition than they had been for many years.

There is no saying how long this régime would have continued if untoward events had not introduced disturbing factors into the situation. No means of organized opposition existed outside of Parliament; individual resistance, however heroic, could effect nothing; no armed rising occurred. If foreign complications could have been avoided, Parliament might have suffered the fate of the French States-General, the meetings of which were suspended from 1614 to 1789. It was the ecclesiastical policy of Charles I and Archbishop Laud that was to prove fatal to the régime—first in Scotland, later in England. It was not very difficult for the Crown to enforce its religious policy upon England—a policy which meant Laud's ideas of episcopacy, ceremony, and Prayer Book. The supremacy over the Church of England was unquestionably vested in the Crown, and the Crown could readily turn the Court of High Commission into an instrument for the enforcement of its religious views upon the clergy and the laity alike. Many Englishmen were devoted to the Church and favourable to the Laudian views; those who did not share these enthusiasms either dissembled, put up with the consequences, or emigrated to a New World; they did not—could not as yet—rebel. But it was quite a different proposition to try to enforce the same ecclesiastical views upon the Scots. In Scotland, ecclesiastical history had taken a different turn from that of England; the majority of the people there had gone very much further in the Puritanical direction than the majority of the people in England; anti-episcopalianism was more rife, Presbyterianism far more developed. Moreover, in Scotland the monarchy had always been decidedly weaker than it had been in England; armed resistance to the Crown had been much commoner than in England. The Scots therefore reacted to Charles's religious policy differently; they rose at once in a widespread revolt, made the National Covenant, and invaded the north of England.

The political *impasse* reached by Charles I at this juncture is revealed by the fact that for the first time in history the English displayed a marked reluctance to fight the inhabitants of the northern kingdom, who now appeared in the unwonted guise of brothers and fellow-sufferers rather than as traditional enemies. Charles could not raise enough men and money to suppress the rebellion, nor even to deal with the invasion, and at long last felt obliged to summon a Parliament once again, in the hope that supplies would be forthcoming for these purposes. The hope was in vain, for the demand of the Commons was for redress of grievances before the grant of supply, and the Short Parliament (13 April to 5 May 1640) was speedily dissolved. The Scottish situation went from bad to worse; the undutiful Scots declared episcopacy to be abolished; the English army was largely mutinous; the army to be imported from Ireland had not arrived; a fresh invasion of Scots occurred. Still futilely hoping to stave off capitulation to the Commons, Charles made ancient ghosts walk by summoning a Great Council of Peers in September, but such of the 'hereditary counsellors of the king' as attended could do nothing but advise temporizing with the Scots pending the assembly of a full Parliament. It was the end of medieval constitutional ambiguity; the monarchy had reached the point where it found itself in fact unable to carry on its government without the Commons in Parliament—the child of its own ambition and will to rule.

When the Long Parliament met on 3 November 1640, no one could have anticipated that it would not finally be dissolved until 16 March 1660. During those twenty years it was to suffer many vicissitudes, but it was to be in the end the sole legal strand running through the turmoil and revolution of Civil War and Interregnum.

Down to August 1641 the members of the Commons were unanimous in pressing measures for the remedy of constitutional grievances, and the king had no practical option but to assent to a number of Acts of Parliament which destroyed the lawful possibility of royal supremacy over the Parliament, and which in effect restored the Tudor balance between the two powers, in so far as this could be established by statute, but at the same time curtailed some of the executive power which the Tudor sovereigns had been wont to exercise. The Triennial Act prescribed that in future not more than three years were to elapse without a meeting of Parliament, and that no Parliament was to be prorogued or dissolved within forty days of assembly without its own consent, whilst another Act provided that the Long Parliament itself was not to be dissolved at all without its own assent. The full implications of this measure were not realized at the time, but the curtailment of the royal prerogative of dissolution was nothing short of revolutionary, and as events turned out it was to be nineteen years before the remnants of the Long Parliament were to come to the point of agreeing to a dissolution. A Tunnage and Poundage Act legalized the prerogative levies that had been made, prohibited them for the future, and made a grant for a short period ahead. Other Acts swept away the prerogative courts (or what were regarded as prerogative courts) of Star Chamber, Court of High Commission, and various others which had of late been used as administrative tribunals enforcing a policy rather than as courts of judicature enforcing the law. Several other Acts put an end to various tortuous methods of raising money recently resorted to by the Crown.

So far reform was on conservative lines, not unacceptable to most shades of opinion other than those of the extreme royalist minority, and a tolerable constitutional scheme had been achieved. The balance thus reached might have been maintained indefinitely, but in fact during the twelve months from August 1641 to August 1642 the political position deteriorated all the way from apparent unanimity to actual civil war. The rot set in, not primarily because of any fundamental differences of constitutional opinion, but essentially because of religious dissension. It was on the question of Church settlement that the Commons could not agree, and the split thus engendered was to give birth before long to the two camps of Roundhead and Cavalier.

One large party in the Commons pressed for the total abolition of episcopacy, the remodelling of the Church on Presbyterian lines, and the revision of the Prayer Book; they went all out for reform of the Church in 'Root and Branch'. The opposing party were not prepared to accept the Presbyterianization of the Church of England on Scottish lines, would not agree to more than a moderate reform of the episcopalian system, and had no enthusiasm for tampering with the Prayer Book. The grave political crisis resulting from this dissension was aggravated by Charles's complete lack of statesmanship, the outbreak of a rebellion in Ireland, which exacerbated anti-Papal and anti-High Church feeling, by rumours of plots and counterplots, by general fear that the king would employ force against the Parliament, by all the ferment and turmoil that arise in situations fraught with unpredictable dangers, in which honest men's minds are divided, the implications of decisive action impossible to foresee, and in which age-long loyalties seem to conflict with conscience and with ambition.

In these circumstances it was doubtless inevitable that episcopalians should become royalists, and Puritans parliamentarians. The Grand Remonstrance, which passed the Commons in November 1641, by a narrow margin of eleven votes, was no more than a piece of party propaganda setting out the programme of the Puritan anti-royalist party, which, among other matters, proposed that the king should employ only such ministers as Parliament might have confidence in. But it was published as an appeal to the nation, and if it did nothing else it served to reveal to the country how divided in mind it had become—a revelation which is a necessary prelude to civil war in a civilized State. The final clash might still have been avoided but for the king's monstrous blunder in going down to the House in person with a large armed guard to attempt to arrest five members of the Commons on the ground that they were in treasonous correspondence with the rebellious Scots. The fact that his attempt was in vain added an element of the ridiculous to a threat of violence which in itself was sufficient to raise the political temperature to boiling point. The capital became too hot to be healthy, and on 10 January 1642 the king left London, never to return save as a prisoner. The Parliament speedily took steps to get control of a military force to counter Charles's open preparations for coercion. When the king refused to assent to a Bill for the transfer of the command of the militia to Parliament, the forms of the Constitution were departed from, and in March the effect of the Militia Bill was decreed by Ordinance of the Houses alone. Both sides hurried on with military preparations, and the Parliamentary ultimatum came in the shape of Pym's Nineteen Propositions of June 1642. The demands were for no less than the surrender by the king of his executive, military, and ecclesiastical powers. No king of England could accede to so fundamental a destruction of the ancient Constitution as this, and Charles rejected the propositions. In July the Parliament set up a Committee of Safety of five peers and ten commoners to exercise executive power, and pressed on with the organization of an army. On 22 August the king raised his standard at Nottingham, and the Civil War had begun.

We cannot concern ourselves here with the course of the war, nor with the details of the several attempts made at establishing a workable constitution during the Interregnum. During the war more than one effort was made to come to an agreement with the king on the crucial constitutional and ecclesiastical questions, but Charles's intransigence, his devotion to the Anglican Church, and his inability to refrain from trying to play one party off against another, even after his military fortunes were irretrievably ruined, together with the emergence of bitter dissensions within the remains of the Parliament itself, resulted in the end in the establishment of the Cromwellian Army as the dominant political force in the country. We cannot trace here how eventually the royal bargain with the Scots over Presbyterianism led to the turning of Cromwell's formidable military machine against his former allies, to the forcible purging of the Commons of the Long Parliament of all but a minority of puppets attached to the Army's strings, to the carrying out of a sentence of death upon 'Charles Stuart, King of England', to the abolition of the monarchy itself and of the House of Lords, and to the establishment of a Commonwealth and Free State in May 1649.

To destroy the framework of civil government was easy, but to build it again was very difficult. Amid the seething welter of parties and sects, political, social, and religious ideas and ideologies that had been let loose by all these events, the only stable element left was the Army and its Captain-General, Oliver Cromwell. It was impossible to secure a firm basis of agreement upon any form of government, and the history of the next eleven years was the history of vain attempts by Cromwell and his friends to clothe the rule of force in constitutional forms, and to establish a civil government equal to the enormous tasks confronting any government at that time. The remnant of the Long Parliament (the Rump) would not dissolve itself, and was forcibly dispersed in April 1653 to make way for a new parliament elected on the novel principle of the divine right of the godly to rule (Barebone's Parliament or the Parliament of Saints, July–December 1653). The more worldly-wise among the saints in this assembly soon tired of its pious and interminable debates, and arranged for the abdication of its pretensions into the hands of the Captain-General. Next a written Constitution (the Instrument of Government of December 1653) was tried, abandoning the idea of the absolute supremacy of a parliament, and reviving an amended Elizabethan monarchy in the form of the Lord Protectorship of Cromwell, limited by a Council of State, and checked by an elective Parliament. But by the irony of history the Lord Protector soon found that he could abide his Parliament as little as Charles Stuart had abided his, and he also found it difficult to get along with his Council of State. By 1657 events had turned so far that the second Parliament of the Protectorate (from which 'undesirable elements' had been carefully excluded) proposed in the Humble Petition and Advice to revive the kingship, to create a nominated Second Chamber, to reduce the Council of State to a mere Privy Council, to authorize a large fixed revenue; in short, to restore something very much like the Constitution of 1641. The Lord Protector accepted the scheme, but there was to be no Cromwellian dynasty. The Army, upon whom Cromwell was dependent for ultimate support, would not stomach the 'title of king', and the Protectorate continued as modified by the other terms of the Humble Petition.

But all was built on shifting sands, and the prevailing republicanism of the next session of the Parliament was countered in the old regal way by an abrupt dissolution. Seven months later, the Lord Protector himself was dead, and from the ensuing confusion, anarchy, and chaos there were no visible means of salvation but to recall to the throne of his ancestors the lawful son and heir of 'Charles Stuart, King of England'. Out of hard and bitter experience Englishmen had come to learn that the remorseless, incalculable power of the past over the present was not to be dispelled by the strivings of a single generation. From 1660 onwards England was never again entirely to forget that the secret of a nation's strength is to have the power of the historic past behind it, not against it.

The Restoration of 1660 was a restoration of the ancient institutions of government, the executive power of the Crown, the legislative and fiscal powers of the House of Lords and the House of Commons, and of the ultimate supremacy of the Common Law; in short, of the Constitution as it had been in August 1641. Ostensibly, the Great Rebellion was effaced from the records, but in reality the events of twenty years are irrevocable, and their deletion was fictitious. True, there was to be no more absolute supremacy of the Crown such as had been manifested during the years 1629–40; nor any absolute supremacy of Parliament such as had been experienced in the years 1641–9; still less was there to be any more military dictatorship such as existed from 1649 to 1660. But the effects and memories of these things could not be expunged, except by the lapse of time. A later generation might forget, but the generation of Charles II could not.

It is therefore not to be wondered at that the Restoration settlement settled little except that the destined path was to be the historic path. No attempt was made to settle the problem of the relations between the restored parts of the Constitution. King, Lords, Commons, and Common Law were left to work out their own salvation; all that had been demonstrated was the indispensability of each. The executive power had been curtailed by the abolition of the administrative tribunals, but the divinity of hereditary right had received much vindication; the rights of Parliament to participate in legislation and taxation had been incontestably confirmed, but Parliament still had no means other than obstructive means of influencing the policy of the executive, which might do much to evade parliamentary obstruction; the supremacy of the Common Law was not questioned, but the judges were still the king's servants, dismissible at pleasure.

No solution of these constitutional difficulties was reached in the reign of Charles II, which resolved itself into a series of political tugs-of-war between the king's party and the opposition party in Parliament, with the money-bags of Louis XIV adding weight mainly but not exclusively on the king's side. What was really new was the outcrop of virulent party politics in and outside of Parliament, which, because they were new, were raw, violent, and crude. The old camps of Cavalier and Roundhead had turned into the Party caucuses of Tories and Whigs, and the old battlefields were converted into wars of political manœuvring. In this form of warfare Charles II was a general as skilful as Cromwell had been in the field, and he fought the political battles of the Crown and of his dynasty with a consummate ability which left him master of the political arena by March 1681. For the remaining four years of his life he ruled without the assistance or hindrance of any Parliament, but he could revive the shades of 1629–40 only by relying upon the liberal financial support of Louis XIV. It was an ignominious way of escape from the equally unscrupulous politics of the Whig opposition. Charles outwitted his opponents, but a government cannot live on its wits for ever, and the suspension of parliamentary methods could hardly have been indefinite.

The death of Charles II in 1685 and the accession of his unadaptable brother, James II, worked, in a very short space of time, a radical change in the political situation. James II, with more than all his father's obstinacy, so conducted himself as to undo in three years all Charles II's work, to place the Crown in a position of political isolation, and to give himself no practical alternative but to emigrate.

For James II was not merely a Roman Catholic, but also so deluded as to deem it possible to reintroduce a Catholic régime, if not with parliamentary assent, then by prerogative power. He was no more bigoted, perhaps, than the Cavalier squires who had reimposed a militant, intolerant Anglicanism at the Restoration, but he should have realized that, if the hands of the clock were to be put back to 1558, they must first pass 1649.

For James II's bigotry was the very one most likely to be unacceptable to all the politically important classes of the nation. The restoration of the Anglican Church had been a cardinal feature of the Restoration of 1660 onwards, and it had been accompanied by the penalization of all Dissenters, Catholic and Protestant alike. The Anglican and Tory squires might reverence the office of king and pay at least lip-service to the doctrines of divine hereditary right and non-resistance to the Crown, but they were not going to have the 'martyrdom' of Charles I brought to naught by his younger son. The Protestant Dissenters wanted relief, but it did not suit them to have it as a gift of the prerogative in despite of parliamentary enactment. And so James II raised up against himself a national opposition of Tories and Whigs, Anglicans and Dissenters, bishops and pastors, an opposition which was united and could only be united in one respect—in a determination to prevent the resurrection of Catholicism and the spread of popery.

We cannot trace here how it was that William, Prince of Orange and Stadtholder of Holland, nephew of James II, and husband of Mary, daughter of James II, having been invited by leaders of both the Tories and the Whigs to deliver the realm in the Protestant interest, was able to sail from Holland, land in Devon, and march on the capital unopposed; how at the last the courage of the Stuarts deserted James II, and how he fled the kingdom, leaving the throne and seat of government vacant. We are more concerned to see how this vacancy was filled.

Settlement by Compromise

The flight of James II left the country with no lawful government, and for the last time it fell to the heirs of the 'common council of the realm', the peers, to meet together to take stock of the situation and to improvise machinery for the re-establishment of a government. With no available king it was impossible to assemble a lawfully constituted Parliament, and recourse was had to the expedient of summoning a Convention consisting of all surviving members of the Parliaments of Charles II. Later an elected Convention Parliament met on 22 January 1689, in which the Tories were in the majority in both Houses, but found themselves split into three sections, each with its own ideas of how to overcome the constitutional difficulties of the situation, whilst the Whigs were unanimous in support of a solution of their own. It was a most fortunate division of 'Party' affiliation, for it made a compromise inevitable. The Tories were naturally gravely embarrassed by the turn events had taken; their cherished doctrines of hereditary divine right and of the duty of non-resistance to the lawful sovereign had become the two horns of a dilemma. If they grasped the former, then James's infant son ought to succeed; but if he did, he too would turn out to be a Catholic monarch, the avoidance of which was the whole purpose of the Revolution. If they grasped the latter, then there was no excuse for the Revolution itself. The Whigs were in no such difficulty. They saw no obstacle to a settlement of the succession by Parliament alone, even by a mere Convention Parliament. Less than a week's debate in the Commons sufficed to bring the moderate Tories into agreement with the Whigs, and to carry two resolutions embodying the essence of the Whig view but couched in such terms as would give the least offence to Tory scruples:

(1) That King James II, having endeavoured to subvert the constitution of his kingdom by breaking the original contract between the king and people; and, by the advice of Jesuits and other wicked persons, having violated the fundamental laws; and having withdrawn himself out of the kingdom, has abdicated the Government; and that the throne is thereby vacant; and

(2) That it hath been found by experience to be inconsistent with the safety and welfare of this Protestant kingdom to be governed by a Popish Prince.

Nobody in the Convention would have wished to contest the second of these propositions, but it was not so easy to pass the first of them through the Lords, where the Tories were in greater strength than in the Commons and did not like the suggestion that the throne could be vacant. It was not practical politics to pretend that James's son was already filling the gap, but the Tory Lords tried to save face by contending that Mary of Orange had automatically succeeded to the throne. A deadlock between the Houses ensued, and was only overcome by the ministering of a strong dose of realism by William himself. He declared that, notwithstanding the esteem he had for his wife, 'he would not hold any thing by apron-strings', and that if this was what was expected of him, he would prefer to return to Holland forthwith. That was a contingency that could not be contemplated by even the most die-hard Tories, and the resolutions of the Commons now instantly passed the Lords. The Prince and Princess of Orange were declared to be the King and Queen of England.

The Convention was converted into the first Parliament of William and Mary, and the old Constitution could function again, with such adjustments as might seem necessary and practicable to avoid any repetition of the coercion of one part of it by another. Any adjustments made had perforce to be the minimum needful to that end, for no adjustments at all could be effected except by agreement among both the Parties; the Whigs must be able to carry a large proportion of the Tories with them; otherwise the attempt would fail. There was therefore to be no doctrinaire reform of the Constitution, no definition of the seat of sovereign power, no talk of the fundamental rights of any power or body within the State. All that was done was to list a number of ways in which James II was deemed to have abused his powers, and to declare these by Act of Parliament to be illegal henceforth.

Once the Bill of Rights had been enacted as a statute on 16 December 1689, no doubt or difficulty remained but that it was illegal for the Crown to suspend the general operation of the laws without parliamentary consent, or to dispense with them in individual cases, or to erect ecclesiastical courts, or to levy money by prerogative without parliamentary grant, or to raise or keep a standing army within the kingdom in time of peace unless with the consent of Parliament. Several other practices of the executive in the past were also specifically declared to be illegal. Shorn of these dozen or so possibilities, it was no longer practicable for the Crown to ride roughshod over the susceptibilities of Parliament. Furthermore, William III of his own motion abandoned the idea that the judges were mere civil servants dismissible at pleasure, and he appointed them during good behaviour. This vital readjustment was subsequently legalized by statute in the Act of Settlement of 1701, which also in effect prescribed that a judge of the High Court could be removed only on an address to the king by both Houses of Parliament. Steps were also taken to modify somewhat the militancy of the Anglican Church, but the Toleration Act of 1689 was not sufficiently tolerant to accord to even Protestant Dissenters more than a relaxation of penalties; their civil disabilities and the absence of any statutory relief for Catholics remained until the nineteenth century.

By 1701 it became necessary to carry the Revolution further by providing for the maintenance of the Protestant succession in the probable contingency that Mary's sister Anne, who would succeed to the throne after the death of William, would have no heir in the direct line to succeed her. The Act of Settlement of 1701 provided that in that event the succession should go to the nearest Protestant representative of the Stuart family, to Sophia, Electress of Hanover, a granddaughter of James I, and her heirs, and that no person who was a Roman Catholic or who married one should succeed, and that the holder of the Crown should join in communion with the Church of England as by law established, and provided also certain safeguards appropriate to the succession of a foreign prince.

The Act of Union of England and Scotland which followed in 1707 was the logical rounding off of the Revolution Settlement, for it was impossible to contemplate a division of the Crowns of the two kingdoms after Anne's death, and the only way to ensure their permanent union was to unite both the Crowns and the two Parliaments, whilst preserving the independence of the other institutions native to the two countries.

The Revolution Settlement thus amounted to no more than the clarification of a few difficult constitutional problems that had been passed over in silence at the Restoration of 1660. The political events and party developments of the thirty years that had intervened had at length made such a clarification possible, and although the settlement was to be in some danger from the Jacobitism of the more extreme Tories and of some of the Highlanders in later years, and still more perhaps from a general lack of enthusiasm for the Hanoverian line, it was never to be undermined or even seriously jeopardized. It was based essentially upon a compromise, and as such was acceptable, not only to the Whigs, but also to the moderate Tories. It could not have been brought about without a revolution, but the revolution was confined to the ousting of the lawful monarch. There was no question henceforth that the king was king by Act of Parliament, and no wistful longings of the Tories for a more divine sanction could make any difference to the plain fact. It was now incontestable, therefore, that in the last resort the Parliament was supreme over the Crown; what Parliament had given, it could take away. But last resorts are not daily medicine, and there was no suggestion that the executive power in the State had been transferred from the Crown to the Parliament. What had been settled once for all was that the Crown had its own proper sphere of authority, that the Houses of Lords and of Commons had theirs, and that the Common Law, too, had its own sphere. The laws which recognized or assumed these co-existent spheres of authority were not going to be altered in any fundamental respect. It remained to adjust the relations between these authorities, and to create working arrangements among them which would answer to the practical needs and political realities of changing circumstances.

4

From the Eighteenth to the Twentieth Century

SINCE THE REVOLUTION SETTLEMENT there have been no fundamental constitutional conflicts in England; there was to be acute controversy and agitation over the reform of Parliament and the extension of the franchise in the early nineteenth century, and not a little disturbance over the modification of the powers of the House of Lords in the early twentieth century, but there were to be no more revolutions. The small adjustments in the ancient Constitution which were made at the Revolution at the end of the seventeenth century, and in the years immediately following, provided a firm and stable framework within which ample room was left for internal changes, which in the course of some two hundred years entirely altered the inner meaning of the constitutional scheme without destroying its fabric. The Revolution confirmed that the government of England was to be a parliamentary limited monarchy; it is that still, but it has also become a constitutional democracy in which the ultimate source of power is the will, not of the Crown, but of the people themselves. This extraordinary metamorphosis was the result of the play of party politics and many fortuitous circumstances during the eighteenth century, still more of the nineteenth century, and was not completed until the twentieth century.

The Separation of Powers, and Government by Influence

The Revolution of 1688–9 bequeathed to the eighteenth century as its form of government a partnership of King, Lords, Commons, and Common Law. The recognition of the independence of the judges left the courts of common law free to arbitrate within the law between the executive and the people, subject only to the overriding supremacy of Acts of Parliament. After 1707 the royal prerogative of refusing assent to Bills passed by both Houses of Parliament was never exercised, so that the two Houses could in effect always alter the law of the land if a majority in both Houses resolved to do so. The Crown still chose the judges, but could no longer dragoon them once they were appointed. The courts therefore were now free to fulfil their destiny, and to apply the law without fear or favour to everyone, ministers and subjects alike, except to the king himself—for the king remained the fountain of justice, and justice cannot do justice upon itself; the king could not be deemed to have authorized an unlawful act, and his servants who committed such an act were alone responsible. The legal rights of the citizens thus received the greatest protection that they can ever receive—the protection of the law enforced by an impartial judiciary.

The exercise of lawful executive power was left vested in the Crown; the ancient rights of the House of Lords to a co-equal legislative power with the House of Commons in all save fiscal matters were also left unimpaired, as well as its supreme appellate jurisdiction in civil litigation. The rights of the House of Commons to discuss any matter whatsoever and to criticize freely the executive power, and its supremacy in financial supply, were assured. The four great and venerable institutions of government, the Crown, the Lords, the Commons, and the Courts of Common Law were thus confirmed in their respective spheres of authority, within which each was largely but not entirely independent of the others. All were mutually indispensable, and none of them in the eighteenth century showed any inclination to attack the position of any other.

It was this marked, although by no means complete, separation of powers that gave to the Constitution of the eighteenth century its character, evoked the admiration of foreign critics, and inspired the framers of the Constitution of the United States of America. The government of 'checks and balances' which resulted from this partial division of powers prevented the absolute supremacy of any one part of the Constitution over another, kept the arena clear for the play of political interests, forces, and parties, and in due course made possible a transformation in the basis of political power.

But it was in the nature of things essential, if the machinery of government was to work tolerably well in practice, to ensure harmonious relations between the executive and the legislature, between the Crown and the Parliament. For the Crown could dissolve Parliament at any time, and Parliament could bring the executive to a stop by refusing financial support and by disbanding the Army. Deadlock between the two powers would mean anarchy, and could not be allowed to happen. It was not allowed to happen, for the Crown had at its disposal the means of ensuring adequately harmonious relations in all normal circumstances. If it could not rely upon the loyal support of majorities in the Houses, it could and did attach to its interest the needful balance of votes in either House by exercising its 'influence'. Party divisions were not as yet clear-cut and all-embracing—indeed, as yet there were no 'Parties' in the modern sense of the term. There were no 'Party' organizations or programmes. There was no clearly definable Tory group or Whig group, even though there were Tory opinions and Whiggish opinions, and diverse shades thereof. Moreover, there were still plenty of members of Parliament who did not think that all wisdom was divided between Tories and Whigs; some conceived it to be their primary duty to support the Crown in Parliament, if necessary against the machinations of group interests, on the principle that 'His Majesty's government must be carried on'; others were willing enough to do so if they saw personal advantage thereby accruing to themselves. The Crown's powers of patronage were ample; the favours, the honours, the pensions, the sinecures it could bestow were great—greater than those within the gift of any of the powerful and wealthy leaders of whichever group happened at any time to be resisting the 'influence' of the Crown.

The link between the executive and the Parliament which was most effective in keeping the wheels of government turning in the eighteenth century and the early nineteenth century was what we would call bribery and corruption, but which then was usually regarded as merely the obvious exercise of 'influence'. It was by the same kind of lubrication that the group interests of the Tories and Whigs were served. The whole system was equivalent to what then represented the 'conventions of the Constitution', without which a Constitution of checks and balances could not be made to work. It was a system necessitated by, and also rendered possible by, the state of parliamentary representation and the electoral franchise.

By the force of economic, social, and other circumstances, by reason of shifting population, and because of the political events of the past generations, most constituencies, both in boroughs and counties, had come to be in practice dominated by the 'interest' of a comparatively small number of great families, large landowners, and wealthy individuals, who in effect could and did secure the election of their own nominees. Few of the lawful electors were in a position to exercise a free choice at an election, even if they had wished to do so. In many boroughs the lawful electors were in fact extremely few in number. The days of popular politics in the modern sense had as yet scarcely dawned, and most elections were decided by family connexions, local interest, and personal advantage. The effective electorate was often very small indeed, and most of the members of Parliament themselves were in reality the nominees of a handful of peers, of large landowners, or of the Crown. Influence and connexion counted for more than party feeling, and when the Crown bid for votes in the House, it was but outbidding or supplementing the influence and connexions of the aristocratic families who dominated the party affiliations of many of the members. That the system in fact produced in Parliament so many men of distinguished talents and abilities as it did need cause no surprise, for it was easier then for young men with little to recommend them but their own merits to secure election than it is under more modern arrangements. A genuine aristocracy always tends to patronize ability, whereas democracy usually tends to patronize mediocrity, for it understands that better.

The logical outcome of this state of affairs was the formation of a Court connexion or party, and this broadly is what happened in the time of George III, from 1760 onwards. There had been King's Friends long before then, but the accidents and vicissitudes of political history during the first half of the century delayed the full development of a tendency which in the circumstances was inevitable. For the notion that the Crown ought to rely upon the support of only one 'Party' or of any particular 'Party' was not one that gained ready or wide acceptance in the conditions of the eighteenth century, and it could for a long time be acceptable only to the 'Party' which stood to gain by so great a token of royal favour and confidence. Both groups had shared in the Revolution, and neither William III nor Anne displayed any marked enthusiasm for granting a monopoly of their confidence to either of the 'Parties', although towards the end of each of their reigns circumstances obliged them to rely mainly upon the Whigs and Tories respectively. But the Tory group split and for half a century ruined itself upon the question of an eleventh-hour restoration of the Stuarts at the very end of Anne's reign, with the result that the Whigs dominated the Parliaments of George I (1714-27) and George II (1727-60). It was this practical circumstance rather than any theory of party government or any particular love of Whiggery that led to the royal choice of predominantly Whig ministers for nearly fifty years after the accession of the Hanoverian line, and of the choice of Sir Robert Walpole as their leader for twenty-one years (1721-42). For the choice of ministers was wholly the king's, and those not very adroit sovereigns, George I and George II, correctly anticipated that on the whole their governments would be carried on with the least trouble to themselves if they relied on the Whiggish interest and let them manage Parliament as best they could with the judicious exercise of the royal patronage. That the royal favour for one group of a particular political complexion lasted so long was to be of importance in the development of the practice of party government and the evolution of the Cabinet, but there was nothing to prevent George III from turning to a rather different arrangement and preferring to be his own chief minister and managing the Commons himself by an appropriate use of his own powers of patronage. It took him ten years to achieve these results, for at the beginning of his reign the services of the masterful William Pitt as a war minister could not be dispensed with, and reliance upon one section or another of the Whigs was temporarily necessary. But from 1770 to 1782, George III, with the assistance of the competent but submissive Lord North, enjoyed the fruits of his efforts and rid himself of the Whig encumbrance. To the fact that his statesmanship was not equal to his powers of management the Constitution of the United States of America owes its origin.

The range of George III's 'influence' did not, for better or for worse, extend to the representative assemblies in the American colonies, but the potency of his influence in the Houses of Parliament set in train forces which in the long run were to diminish the sovereign's ability to exercise government personally, to undermine both the reason for and the possibility of an indefinite continuance of patronage as the effective link between the executive and the legislature, and to encourage the growth of the principles of responsible Party government which finally were to place the Crown beyond politics altogether. For the Whiggish connexion, or part of it, ousted from royal favour, began to form a genuine opposition based on political principles which, when in the fullness of time they could be carried into effect, would modify the reality of the royal influence by drastically curtailing its rights of patronage, and would eventually destroy the basis of government by 'influence' by securing the thorough reform of the House of Commons itself.

When, by the end of 1783, George III rid himself of the makeshift ministries that ensued after Lord North's resignation in 1782, and by his favour procured a great 'Tory' majority behind the younger Pitt, the Crown had unwittingly given a strong impetus to government by Party. For there was now to be a Tory ascendancy comparable in length and completeness with that of the Whigs in the earlier half of the century, and although royal favour was to continue for at least a generation to be indispensable to the formation of any particular ministry, nearly all future governments were to be primarily Party governments. The importance of the link of 'influence' therefore declined, but still remained essential, for there was to be no reform of Parliament until 1832.

The Reform of Parliament

A number of serious proposals for the reform of Parliament were mooted towards the end of the eighteenth century, but the reaction of political opinion to the French Revolution and the long-drawn-out struggle of the Napoleonic wars delayed the successful fruition of the movement until 1832. The delay was lengthy, not only because of reactionary political feeling, but also because of the inevitable doubts and fears of those who were more concerned that the government should be effectively carried on than that apparent anomalies in the representation of the people should be corrected. For more than a hundred years, the executive had been enabled to function only by managing the House of Commons, and reform of the House would manifestly destroy the basis of that management. The anxious question put by the Duke of Wellington, the leader of the Tories in the Lords, when confronted by the Reform Bill of 1832, epitomizes perfectly, not only this point of view, but also the true historical significance of the Reform Bill itself. 'How', he asked, 'is the king's government to be carried on, if the Bill passes?'

That, indeed, was the question, for the ultimate solution to the problem—the exercise in the king's name of the executive powers by a Cabinet of ministers who should in effect be the nominees of the majority Party returned to the House of Commons by the electorate—was not as yet consciously envisaged. Although various suggestive precedents for some such arrangements existed, no one as yet contemplated a situation in which the ministers of the Crown could dispense with the king's favour, monopolize his political activity, and rely solely upon Party allegiance in the Commons, backed by the 'feeling in the country'. In the legal sense, the principle of ministerial responsibility had already made possible the principle of royal irresponsibility, but the two principles had not as yet been combined in the political sense.

The recession of the king from politics and the advance of the principles of Cabinet government were both slow processes, and necessarily conditioned by the successive steps in the reform of Parliament and the extension of the electoral franchise taken during the nineteenth and twentieth centuries. The ultimate result of these developments was to upset the balance of powers characteristic of the eighteenth-century Constitution, and to concentrate dominant power in the House of Commons and its 'executive committee', the Cabinet.

The Reform Act of 1832 was not passed without much political agitation, prolonged crisis, and the application of great political pressure upon the House of Lords and upon the king, William IV. In the end the Crown was obliged to promise to create sufficient peers to ensure a majority for the Bill in the Upper House, but William IV's action in privately advising the Duke of Wellington to induce his fellow Tories in the Lords to abstain from voting against the Bill obviated the necessity for implementing the promise. The Bill passed and received the royal assent on 7 June 1832.

The whole episode was in reality a great step forward in the principles of Cabinet government, for the king's attempt at commissioning a Tory government under the Iron Duke in despite of the great majority of the Whigs in the House of Commons, and of the manifest will of the people expressed in no uncertain manner during the preceding election, proved a complete failure, and Wellington himself was obliged to advise the king to recall Earl Grey and his Whigs to office. In this sense 1832 represents a landmark in the change-over from government by influence to government by Party, but the terms of the Reform Act itself, although of fundamental importance, were of a comparatively modest character. The disfranchisement of most of the boroughs which had become 'rotten' through the decay of their populations or which had come to be 'in somebody's pocket', and the transference of their seats to newer centres of population, were of more immediate importance than the measures which increased the electorate by about 50 per cent, for there was to be no secret ballot until 1873. Much local influence therefore continued to be exerted at elections.

The extensions of the franchise made in 1832 were of a very limited character, were strictly related to property or its occupation, and in no sense established a democratic electorate. The type and composition of ensuing Houses of Commons continued therefore to be very similar to those normal before 1832. But none the less a great triumph of the popular will over the vested interests of the Crown and the governing class had taken place, and henceforth no government in power could afford to ignore the views either of the limited electorate or of the people who might some day come within the charmed circle of the electorate itself. For reform was now the thing, and it was not long before a spate of great reforming Acts of Parliament began to clear up the accumulated anomalies of centuries. The legislative potentiality of the ancient Parliament at last came to fruition, and has ever since been steadily applied to the tasks of bringing almost all the institutions of national life into better harmony with public opinion.

The next step in parliamentary reform came in 1867, when Disraeli 'dished the Whigs' by carrying a measure to improve the distribution of seats and to extend the franchise further. By the widening of the property and occupation of property qualifications, a million new voters were enfranchised and nearly doubled the size of the electorate. The increase was mainly among the 'respectable' artisan class of the towns, and the urban workers who were not householders and the rural workers generally were still left out. The new electorate remained only a small proportion of the total male population, but the doubling of the voters could not be without its effect upon the House of Commons, which began to be swayed more by Party programmes, and to conceive itself more directly responsible to the electorate than it had in the past; the modern tendency of members to act less like the attorneys and more like the delegates of their constituents made its appearance.

The Acts of 1832 and 1867 had not been accompanied by any of the disastrous consequences foretold by gloomy political prophets, nor did the introduction of the secret ballot by a Gladstonian Act of 1873 bring the world to an end. Her Majesty's Government was still able to function, and the three further Representation of the People Acts of 1884, 1918, and 1928, although far more sweeping in effect than their precursors, were passed with progressively diminishing opposition. Gladstone's Act of 1884 reduced the occupation of premises qualification almost but not quite to vanishing point, increased the electorate by nearly a further 70 per cent, bringing it up to rather more than four and a quarter millions. A Redistribution Act of the following year made radical changes in the distribution of seats and the delimitation of constituencies, making them less like the ancient organic communities and more like arithmetical divisions of population.

It was the nature of the war of 1914–18 that brought about the next and still more drastic extension of the franchise. The war was not fought by men and women qualified to fight by property or the occupation of premises, and Lloyd George's Bill for extending the franchise to all men of twenty-one years of age resident in a constituency for a short, prescribed period, and to women of thirty years of age subject to certain prescribed conditions, passed by an overwhelming majority. Further redistribution of seats was effected, and sex as a disqualification for membership of the Commons was abolished. The Act added no fewer than thirteen millions to the register of voters, bringing it up to twenty-one millions, but carefully avoided allowing the preponderance of women in the population to be reflected in the electorate. For ten years the citadel of male superiority was held, but capitulated with Baldwin's Act of 1928, which reduced the qualification for registration as a voter to the simple attainment of twenty-one years of age and short residence in the constituency, added eight more millions[1] to the electorate, and, the structure of the population being what it was, gave the balance of voting power to a million and three-quarters of 'surplus women'. The two further Acts of 1945 and 1948 abolished all forms of plural voting, and established as the sole qualifications for the vote the attainment of the age of twenty-one years, residence in a particular place on the qualifying date (10 October), and registration on the electoral roll, a new one of which comes into force on 16 February each year. Thus, in less than a century, democratic theory had carried the reform of the franchise to its logical extreme.

[1] The last electoral register (1965) stood at just under thirty-six millions.

The Rise of Cabinet Government

Just as in the study of the early history of Parliament the issues are confused by the fact that the term 'parliament' was for long used in a sense quite different from that of modern usage, so in the early history of the Cabinet the name and the thing existed long before Cabinet government in the modern sense had made any appreciable development. The earliest Cabinets of ministers of the Restoration period were no more than committees of the Privy Council; in time Cabinets ceased to be such, and became in effect, though never in form, committees of the Houses of Parliament, and in the long run of the predominant Party in the Commons. The Cabinet has always remained outside the law, and Blackstone was able to write his famous *Commentaries on the Laws of England* (1765), including an account of the Constitution of his day, without even a passing reference to any such body. But in the hundred years that elapsed between that date and the publication in 1865 by Walter Bagehot of the first of his articles, subsequently issued as his book *The English Constitution*, the principles of Cabinet government had developed to so great a degree that they formed the dominant theme in his exposition. It is true that Bagehot probably underrated the extent to which royal influence in politics still lingered at that time, but he was justified in believing that in his day the 'efficient secret' of the Constitution had come to be 'the close union, the nearly complete fusion of the executive and legislative powers', brought about by the 'connecting link' of the Cabinet—a 'new word' by which was meant 'a committee of the legislative body selected to be the executive body'.

But in its origins the Cabinet was nothing of the kind. At the Restoration, as we have seen, executive power remained vested solely in the king, assisted by a Privy Council appointed wholly by him. But the Privy Council was a large body, some of whose members held honorific posts carrying little or no administrative responsibility, whilst the home and foreign policies of Charles II were such as eminently required the assistance of a more secretive and exclusive body than the Privy Council as a whole could provide. Charles II and his successors therefore found it expedient to confine their fullest confidence to a small selection of chosen ministers, in so far as they were prepared to give full confidence to anyone. Committees of the Privy Council had existed for one purpose or another from the sixteenth century, and some of these formed the nuclei of Departments of State; some continue to exist today; but a peculiar destiny awaited the informal committee of the Privy Council which comprised the ministers in whom the king reposed most confidence and admitted to the inmost place in his counsels. It soon became realized by contemporaries that effective power, which then meant primacy of place in the king's estimation, had passed from the Privy Council as a whole to a small body variously known as 'the Committee', 'the Cabal', 'the Junto', 'the Cabinet Council', or 'the Cabinet'. It was not a development viewed with favour, and the framers of the Act of Settlement of 1701 sought to put an end to it by providing that all matters of state proper to the Privy Council according to the laws and customs of the realm should be transacted therein, and that all resolutions reached in the Council should be signed by the councillors advising and consenting thereto, and, further, that no person holding an office or place of profit under the king or receiving a pension from the Crown should be eligible for membership of the House of Commons. But the necessities of government and the force of circumstances were too strong to be obstructed by reactionary legislation of this kind; moreover, by this time the old fear of the executive was being superseded by its manifest dependence upon the goodwill of the legislature, and replaced by the political ambitions of the Commons to influence it as much as possible. The first two of these provisions were repealed in 1705, before they became operative, and the third was modified at an early date to the extent of allowing ministers of the Crown to be re-elected to the House after accepting office.

By the time of the accession of George I, it was generally recognized that the Privy Council had been superseded as the effective governing body by a Cabinet of persons holding high office in State, Church, or royal Household, and at times at least by an inner ring of ministers of major responsibilities in the more particular confidence of the king. The eighteenth century passed before the composition of the Cabinet came to be confined to the ministerial heads of the principal Departments of State, and it remained for Addington in 1801 to point out to Lord Loughborough, who had been Lord Chancellor in the preceding Cabinet, that his continued attendance at meetings of the new Cabinet was undesirable.

Just as the Cabinet has remained outside the cognizance of the law, so has the office of Prime Minister,[1] and the term 'Prime

[1] Except as indicated above, p. 17.

Minister', like the term 'Cabinet', began as a term of abuse and reproach. It was not in harmony with the old traditions that any one minister should appear to monopolize the confidence of the king or stand in his especial favour, and when, after the Restoration, circumstances in fact tended to point to one of the members of the Cabinet as its leading member, he was sometimes alluded to in derision as a 'prime minister'. The Lord Treasurer, or, when the Treasury was put into commission, the First Lord of the Treasury, usually attracted to himself this appellation, and it was no accident that the holder of this legal office should acquire primacy of place, for it was he who was best able to control the flow of royal patronage, and therefore to exercise the arts of management. It is often said that Sir Robert Walpole was the first modern Prime Minister, but in fact he was called so only by his enemies, and he himself repudiated the title. Moreover, he was in any case far too dependent upon royal favour for the continuance of his office to be a Prime Minister in anything like the modern sense. There could be no Prime Minister in the modern sense whilst the king himself remained the ultimate director of policy, nor until the Cabinet and the principles of Party and Cabinet government had become consolidated into something like their modern form. In 1803 William Pitt found it worth while to declare that it was 'an absolute necessity in the conduct of the affairs of this country that there should be an avowed and real minister possessing chief weight in the Council and the principal place in the confidence of the king. The power must rest in the person generally called First Minister.' Perhaps Sir Robert Peel was the minister who first found himself (from 1841) in a position which closely resembled that of a modern Prime Minister, even if the title was not officially used until the last quarter of the nineteenth century, and the office received no official precedence until 1905, when by royal warrant the Prime Minister was placed next after the Archbishop of York.

If the consolidation of the Cabinet as a body of responsible ministers was slow, so also was the decline of its dependence upon the royal favour and the recession of the Crown from politics, which were necessary developments before either the Cabinet or the Prime Minister could assume their modern positions. The younger Pitt, after eighteen years of office, was obliged by George III's obstinate refusal to agree to Catholic emancipation in Ireland to resign, notwithstanding that he had a large majority behind him in the Commons. Until George IV yielded in 1829, no ministry could proceed with that issue. In 1834 William IV dismissed Lord Melbourne and commissioned Sir Robert Peel to form a ministry, notwithstanding that at that juncture Peel had the support of only a quarter of the House. In 1839 Peel, although he then had a majority behind him, could not persuade the very young Queen Victoria to make the changes in her Household appointments which he deemed politically necessary, and she entrusted the more favoured Melbourne with an administration which lasted for two years despite his Party's minority in the House. But by 1841 Peel carried a resolution that 'it is at variance with the spirit of the Constitution for a ministry to continue in office without the confidence of the House'. The Queen could not keep Peel out of office any longer, and royal favour alone no longer sufficed to maintain a ministry in office.

Royal influence in politics thereafter declined, but did not vanish until the end of the century, possibly not until the twentieth century. Indeed, it could not vanish until the extension of the electorate and the development of Party politics came to play a decisive part in political life, nor until the Crown was obliged by circumstances to grant dissolutions of Parliament without regard to the prospects of success for an administration which it happened to prefer.

For over twenty years after the fall of Peel in 1846 no general election gave a decisive majority to any one Party, and it was consequently inevitable that the duty of finding a workable government should fall upon the Queen; the minority governments of 1846–52, 1858–9, and 1866–8, and the coalition of 1852–5 could not otherwise have come into existence at all. Not until 1868 was the decision of a general election so clear as to cause the government in office to resign without waiting for a division in the House. In the absence of clear electoral majorities, the exercise of the discretion of the Crown in selecting a ministry was the only means of procuring any government. But when decisive electoral verdicts were given, the Queen could not, even if she had wished, resist them, and there was no practical alternative to the commissioning of Peel in 1841, of Gladstone in 1868 and 1880, of Disraeli in 1874. The Queen, however, retained a strong influence upon the composition of Cabinets, and as late as 1895 had to be persuaded by the opposition leader to refrain from insisting on a dissolution contrary to the advice of her responsible ministers;

nor was she unduly diffident in making known her views on political questions.

But the day of active direction of politics by the Crown passed with the Victorian Age itself. When in the reign of Edward VII (1901–10) it was rumoured that the king was opposed to any change in free trade, and the sovereign issued an announcement that 'The King never expresses any opinion on political matters except on the advice of his responsible ministers, and therefore the statement must be inaccurate', the Crown had become removed from politics. But there are good grounds for supposing that George V (1910–36) was the first sovereign who fully accepted the principles of constitutional monarchy in the modern sense of the term, and these have been faithfully followed by his successors.[1]

The king had now assumed for nearly all purposes the impersonality of the Crown, but remained entrusted with sufficient discretionary powers in the last resort to ensure the carrying on of His Majesty's Government and the continuous working of the Constitution, and with a capacity limited only by circumstances to act as a consultant towards a Cabinet of ministers who had become responsible only to the law for their deeds, and only to the electorate through the House of Commons for their policies.

[1] Information upon the relations between the sovereigns and Cabinets is provided by the official lives of George V and of George VI, by Sir Harold Nicolson (1952) and by Sir John Wheeler-Bennett (1958) respectively.

Epilogue

IN OUR SURVEY of the present-day Constitution in Chapter 1 above, a formula was set out[1] which attempted to express briefly the essence of the modern Constitution. That formula in its entirety could not with accuracy have been applied to the description of the Constitution at any time prior to the second, or even perhaps the third, decade of the twentieth century. None the less, the factors which together make up the formula are the products of many centuries of history. All the ages of English history have contributed something to the present-day Constitution, which could not be what it is if those remoter times had contributed elements different from those which in fact they did contribute.

To find the origins and to understand the significance of the kingship, we must retrace our steps through all the long centuries of our history, and even beyond into the dim lights of prehistory among the Anglo-Saxon immigrants. To discover the beginnings of Parliament, we must look first for the origins of the House of Lords, going back to the council of feudal tenants-in-chief of the Norman conquerors, perhaps even to the assemblies of the wise men in the ancient kingdoms before the unification of England, as well as to the king's intimates and officers of his court, without whom no king of any age could govern; we must also hark back to the days of King John, Henry III, and Edward I before we can perceive whence came the House of Commons, and back further still to beyond the Norman Conquest to trace the part played in government by the ordinary free man. The universal electoral franchise of today is of only very recent creation, but representatives of local communities were being chosen to come to meet the

[1] See above, pp. 8–9.

king's government at the centre seven hundred years ago. The faithful Commons are half as old as England itself.

Cabinet government in the modern sense is comparatively recent, but the Crown has made use of a Cabinet of ministers since the time of Charles II, and has used ministers, councillors, and advisers of one kind or another since the earliest times of royal government. The political responsibility of Ministers to the electorate as we now understand it is not a very long-established principle, but it is the result of struggles of many generations to impose upon His Majesty's servants responsibility to opinion other than that of the king alone, and in a different form it goes back to a time before Parliament and before a House of Commons existed at all. The responsibility of Ministers to the law is a notion central to the whole course of our legal history, and the machinery for its enforcement was devised long before modern democracy was thought of, and His Majesty's judges were enforcing it before there were any Right Honourable gentlemen. The modern Civil Service is mainly nineteenth-century in its present form, but it is the lineal descendant of the clerks and officials whom the earliest kings gathered together in their Households to do their bidding and to carry out the daily tasks of government.

Our modern Constitution is thus a heritage from the past, and in it the institutions, the devices, and the ideals of many centuries are embodied and fused into a great and effective instrument of government. The twentieth century has already made its contributions to the law and conventions of the Constitution, and some of these will doubtless prove to be permanent. It has achieved fresh ideals of monarchy, and fully developed the principles of Cabinet government; it has defined and modified the relations between the House of Lords and the House of Commons; it has extended the franchise to the whole adult population in accordance with modern democratic ideas; it has enormously increased the powers of the executive, and thereby reduced the effectiveness of Parliament as against His Majesty's Government.

The most significant of these developments is the expansion of executive power. This has been due in part to the exigencies of the long struggle to survive against the menace of external enemies that has been imposed upon the State during most of the first half of the twentieth century; and in part to changing conceptions of the proper functions and scope of government itself. The conditions created by war, rumours of war, and the aftermaths of war will perhaps not last for ever, and social and economic theories are usually transient and inevitably modified in the light of experience. What balance of powers among the authorities within the Constitution will become stabilized in normal circumstances no one can pretend to say, for no one can predict what circumstances will become normal in the last decades of the century.

It is a manifest lesson of all our history—and indeed of any history—that an excessive growth of executive power is inimical to the liberties of the individual citizen, but whether the modern electorate is as yet sufficiently experienced in the wise exercise of its sovereign power to apply that lesson remains to be seen. The elasticity of the English Constitution is one of its greatest merits, but it is also a source of some danger, for the ease with which the Constitution can be amended and modified tends to obscure the significance and consequences of changes which may be slight in themselves, but which may be of profound accumulative effect. Knowledge as well as eternal vigilance is the price of liberty.

What is certain is that the law and conventions of the Constitution will continue to change in response to the real or fancied needs of the present and future generations. Changing conditions may require changing methods of government and the creative energies of the nation are not easily exhausted. We have achieved universal suffrage and the sovereignty of the common people, but these things are not in themselves the Promised Land nor the panacea of all evils.

For the Promised Land always turns out to be a mirage beckoning men on towards the unknown and the unforeseen, and panaceas often turn out to be quack remedies. No man can foretell whether our Constitutional Democracy will succeed in remaining true to its fundamental ideals and maintain a just balance between law and liberty, progress and stability, the State and the individual. We can understand something of the historic past, and the present is always with us, but the past and present contingencies which together will shape and eventually determine the future are for ever elusive.

Select Bibliography

Chapter 1

THE best general text-book of present-day constitutional law is that by E. C. S. Wade and G. G. Phillips, *Constitutional Law* (6th ed. 1960). A larger work, containing a certain amount of not always very reliable historical explanation, is Sir W. Anson, *Law and Custom of the Constitution*, first published 1886–92, vol. I, 5th ed. by Sir M. L. Gwyer (1922); vol. II, 4th ed. by A. Berriedale Keith (1935). A. V. Dicey's *Introduction to the Study of the Law of the Constitution* is a classical exposition which has had a fundamental influence upon conceptions of the Constitution. First published in 1885, it has not yet been superseded, but it is in some important respects out of date, and it should be read with the critical introduction to the 10th ed. (1959) by E. C. S. Wade.

W. I. Jennings's *Cabinet Government* (2nd ed. 1951) and *Parliament* (1939) are two admirable and exhaustive studies of those institutions as they operated at the dates of publication. *Parliament: A Survey*, ed. Lord Campion (1952), is useful for more recent developments. There is a growing literature on the difficult and rather technical problems of delegated legislation and judicial decision. The best introduction to the subject is H. W. R. Wade, *Administrative Law* (1961), together with Sir Cecil Carr's *Concerning English Administrative Law* (1941) and Sir Carleton Allen's *Bureaucracy Triumphant* (1931). The latter's *Law and Orders* (1945) is a fuller study, but is somewhat marred by an excessively legalistic point of view and ill-balanced criticism of bureaucracy. H. E. Dale's *The Higher Civil Service of Great Britain* (1941) is a valuable account of the pre-war Civil Service from the inside. H. G. Hanbury, *English Courts of Law* (1944, 4th ed. prepared by D. C. M. Yardley 1967), in this Series, gives a useful survey of the judiciary. C. S. Emden, *The People and the Constitution* (1933) offers valuable information and discussion of various themes of special interest to the modern electorate. D. N. Chester, *The Nationalised Industries* (2nd ed. 1951) analyses the statutory provisions in this field. W. A. Robson, *Nationalised Industry and Public Ownership* (1960) provides a thorough study of its subject, and a valuable discussion is in

A. H. Hanson, *Parliament and Public Ownership* (1961). Useful short surveys of contemporary constitutional developments are published annually in *Parliamentary Affairs*, the journal of the Hansard Society.

Chapters 2–4

A comprehensive select bibliography of *English Constitutional History* is provided by S. B. Chrimes and I. A. Roots (Historial Association Helps for Students of History, No. 58, 1958).

There is not at present any very satisfactory general survey of English Constitutional History in one volume. A completely revised and largely rewritten edition by T. F. T. Plucknett of an old and hitherto very indifferent text-book, T. P. Taswell-Langmead's *English Constitutional History* (11th ed. 1960), goes far to fill the gap. G. Smith, *A Constitutional and Legal History of England* (1955) offers a useful general survey, especially suitable for American readers. F. W. Maitland, *The Constitutional History of England* (1908) and G. B. Adams's *Constitutional History of England* (1922, new ed. 1934) to some extent supplement each other, and should be read together. The former consists of posthumously published lectures by one of our greatest historians and, being primarily legal in its standpoint, it strengthens the narrative and political point of view of the latter. Both, however, are somewhat out of date on many themes. A useful survey is provided by B. Lyon, *A Constitutional and Legal History of Medieval England* (1960). More detailed surveys are contained in J. E. A. Jolliffe's *The Constitutional History of Medieval England* (4th ed. 1961) and D. L. Keir's *The Constitutional History of Modern Britain* (6th ed. 1960). The latter is a thoroughly sound and readable text-book, but the former is less well adapted to the needs of beginners, although containing many expositions of great interest. An extensive collection of original documents translated or printed in modern English, with most useful bibliographical references, is provided by C. Stephenson and F. G. Marcham, *Sources of English Constitutional History* (1938).

Chapter 2

F. M. Powicke's *Medieval England* (1931) in the Home University Library provides an admirable introduction to the general subject, largely from the constitutional point of view. W. Stubbs's *The Constitutional History of England* (1874–8; 5th ed. 1891–6) remains the classic exposition of the subject for the Middle Ages, but it is very much out of date both in its assumptions and much of its substance, especially for the earlier period, and is therefore to be used with caution. C. Petit-Dutaillis and G. Lefebvre, *Studies and Notes Supplementary to Stubbs's Constitutional History* (1930), are indispensable for reading in conjunction with Stubbs, together with many later contributions, mentioned in the above recent text-books. Still more recent and valuable correctives to Stubbs as well as important cognate contributions are to be found in H. G. Richardson and G. O. Sayles, *The Governance of England from the Conquest to Magna Carta* (1963).

The masterly *History of English Law before the time of Edward I* (1898) by Sir F. Pollock and F. W. Maitland, written in a superb style, together with Sir W. Holdsworth's *History of English Law*, vols. I (7th revised ed. 1956) and II (3rd ed. 1922–3), are works of the first rank, invaluable for the legal side of the subject.

T. F. T. Tout's *Chapters in Medieval Administrative History* (1930–8) are a mine of information on the practical workings of government, a general survey of which is provided by S. B. Chrimes, *An Introduction to the Administrative History of Mediaeval England* (3rd revised ed. 1966).

More detailed information on the themes with which they deal may be pursued in such works as: F. M. Stenton, *The First Century of English Feudalism* (2nd ed. 1961); R. L. Poole, *The Exchequer in the Twelfth Century* (1912); J. E. A. Jolliffe, *The Angevin Kingship* (1955); W. S. McKechnie, *Magna Carta* (2nd ed. 1914); J. C. Holt, *Magna Carta* (1965); F. Thompson, *Magna Carta: its role in the making of the English Constitution, 1300–1629* (1948); W. L. Warren, *King John* (1961); F. J. West, *The Justiciarship in England, 1066–1232* (1966); W. A. Morris, *The Medieval English Sheriff to 1300* (1927); D. Pasquet, *Essays on the Origins of the English House of Commons*, English ed. by R. G. D. Laffan and G. T. Lapsley (1925); A. B. White, *Self-Government at the King's Command* (1933); R. F. Treharne, *The Baronial Plan of Reform, 1258–63* (1932); B. Wilkinson, *Studies in the Constitutional History of the Thirteenth and Fourteenth Centuries* (1937); M. V. Clarke, *Medieval Representation and Consent* (1936); S. B. Chrimes, *English Constitutional Ideas in the Fifteenth Century* (1936).

The main works of Sir John Fortescue are available in the edition of his *De Laudibus Legum Angliae* by S. B. Chrimes (1942) and of his *The Governance of England* by C. Plummer (1885).

Representative documents in the original languages are to be found in W. Stubbs, *Select Charters and Other Illustrations of English Constitutional History to 1307* (9th ed. by H. W. C. Davis, 1913), and S. B. Chrimes and A. L. Brown, *Select Documents of English Constitutional History, 1307–1485* (1961).

Chapter 3

Sir William Holdsworth's *History of English Law*, vols. IV and VI (1929), provide a valuable general survey of the constitutional history of the Tudor and Stuart periods. J. R. Tanner's *Tudor Constitutional Documents* (1922) was a fine collection but has now been replaced by G. R. Elton, *The Tudor Constitution* (1961), with succinct and lucid commentaries, and G. W. Prothero's *Select Statutes and Other Constitutional Documents Illustrative of the Reigns of Elizabeth and James I* (1891) is also valuable for its preface. K. W. M. Pickthorn's *Early Tudor Government* (1934) illuminates the practical working of government. Invaluable studies are G. R. Elton, *The Tudor Revolution in Government* (1953) and Sir John Neale, *The Elizabethan House of Commons* (1949) and *Elizabeth I and her Parliaments*, 2 vols. (1953 and 1957). Important themes are dealt with in more detail in C. A. Beard, *The Office of Justice of the Peace in England* (1904) and F. M. G. Evans, *The Principal Secretary of State, 1558–1680* (1923). Sir Thomas Smith, *De Republica Anglorum* (in English), ed. L. Alston (1906), is representative of Elizabethan constitutional theory.

J. R. Tanner's *English Constitutional Conflicts of the Seventeenth Century* (1928) is a useful even though in some respects out-of-date survey of the subject, and a still more recent exposition is to be found in M. A. Thomson, *A Constitutional History of England, 1642–1801* (1938). A valuable fresh study is Margaret Judson, *The Crisis of the Constitution, 1603–1642* (1949). Documents for the period are available in J. R. Tanner, *Constitutional Documents of the Reign of James I* (1930), S. R. Gardiner, *Constitutional Documents of the Puritan Revolution* (3rd ed. 1906), and J. P. Kenyon, *The Stuart Constitution, 1603–1688* (1965).

E. Jenks is informative in *The Constitutional Experiments of the Commonwealth* (1890). G. M. Trevelyan, *The English Revolution* (in the Home University Library, 1938) is valuable, and may be supplemented by I. Deane Jones, *The English Revolution* (1931). Developments in the executive may be followed in M. A. Thomson, *The Secretaries of State, 1681–1782* (1932).

Chapter 4

Vol. X of Sir W. Holdsworth's *History of English Law* (1938) is wholly devoted to the constitutional history of the eighteenth century and is the best general survey available, continued up to 1832 in vol. XIII (1952). A more popular account is contained in M. A. Thomson's *Constitutional History* mentioned above, and documents and commentary are provided in E. N. Williams, *The Eighteenth Century Constitution, 1688–1815* (1960). Sir T. E. May's *The Constitutional History of England since the accession of George III* (1861–3), continued to 1911 by F. Holland (1912), remains valuable for a number of themes within the period it covers. Sir W. Blackstone's *Commentaries on the Laws of England* (1765) are available in several editions. W. Bagehot's *The English Constitution* (1865, 2nd ed. 1872) may conveniently be read in The World's Classics edition. Subjects of major importance are dealt with in detail in A. S. Turberville, *The House of Lords in the Eighteenth Century* (1927); L. B. Namier, *The Structure of Politics at the accession of George III* (1929); R. Pares, *George III and the Politicians* (1953); E. and A. Porrit, *The Unreformed House of Commons* (1909); G. S.

Veitch, *The Genesis of Parliamentary Reform* (1913); J. R. M. Butler, *The Passing of the Great Reform Bill* (1914).

A mass of material relating to the executive is collected in E. R. Turner, *The Privy Council of England in the Seventeenth and Eighteenth Centuries* (1927–8) and *The Cabinet Council of England in the Seventeenth and Eighteenth Centuries* (1930–2). A. Berriedale Keith, *British Cabinet Government* (2nd ed. by N. H. Gibbs, 1952) is invaluable, and the same authority's *The Constitutional History of England from Queen Victoria to George VI* (1940) analyses its subject exhaustively. A fresh study is J. P. Mackintosh, *The British Cabinet* (1962). K. B. Smellie, *A Hundred Years of English Government* (1937) provides a helpful and suggestive survey. Illustrative documents are to be found in Sir C. G. Robertson, *Select Statutes, Cases, and Documents to illustrate English Constitutional History, 1660–1894* (ed. of 1935); D. L. Keir and F. H. Lawson, *Cases on Constitutional Law* (2nd ed. 1933); C. S. Emden, *Select Speeches on the Constitution* (1939); W. C. Costin and J. S. Watson, *The Law and Working of the Constitution, 1660–1914*, 2 vols. (1952); G. le May, *British Government 1914–1953: Select Documents* (1955).

Index